23 Paul's sermons at Lystra & Athens
diff from those to Jews

THREE CRUCIAL DECADES

THREE

CRUCIAL DECADES

Studies in the Book of Acts

Floyd V. Filson

JOHN KNOX PRESS Richmond, Virginia

Library of Congress Catalog Card Number: 63-15197

Scripture quotations are from the Revised Standard Version, copyright 1946 and 1952 by the Division of Christian Education of the National Council of the Churches of Christ in the United States of America.

© M. E. Bratcher 1963

Printed in the United States of America

9186

FOREWORD

The chapters of this book present in slightly revised form the Smyth Lectures delivered at Columbia Theological Seminary, Decatur, Georgia, on November 5-9, 1962. I am grateful to President Richards and the Faculty for the invitation to give the Smyth Lectures, and I remember with great appreciation the friendly welcome I received during the week I spent on the campus of the Seminary.

The study of the book of Acts involves a multitude of problems, and a series of five lectures could not discuss such issues in detail. My aim has been to sketch a general picture of the rise and development of the church during the three crucial decades with which the church began. Perhaps the chief test which any picture of those earliest years must pass is whether the sketch gives a consistent and convincing account of the emergence and expansion of apostolic Christianity. I have tried to present such an account.

Since such a method of presentation does not include a running debate with alternate views, it may be well to indicate the most important modern works for a thorough study of the book of Acts. Indispensable is the noted five-volume work, *The Beginnings of Christianity. Part I. The Acts of the Apostles,* edited by F. J. Foakes Jackson and Kirsopp Lake (London:

Macmillan and Co., Limited, 1920-1933). An outstanding contributor to this classic work was Henry J. Cadbury, whose book on *The Making of Luke-Acts* (New York: The Macmillan Company, 1927) is one of the most helpful aids in the study of Acts. A conservative and thoroughly scholarly work is the commentary on *The Acts of the Apostles* by F. F. Bruce (London: The Tyndale Press, 1951). Those who read German will find the most thorough recent introduction and commentary in the too rigidly critical German work by E. Haenchen, *Die Apostelgeschichte* (Göttingen: Vandenhoeck & Ruprecht, 1956).

Surveys and discussions of the chief problems in the study of Acts are provided by W. L. Knox, *The Acts of the Apostles* (Cambridge: The University Press, 1948), and C. K. Barrett, *Luke the Historian in Recent Study* (London: The Epworth Press, 1961). For those who read French there is a masterly survey and evaluation of the study of Acts since 1800 by Étienne Trocmé, *Le "Livre des Actes" et l'histoire* (Paris: Presses Universitaires de France, 1957).

Literary and stylistic studies receive a fresh treatment in the essays of Martin Dibelius, *Studies in the Acts of the Apostles* (English translation, London: SCM Press, 1956).

I have learned much from these and from scores of other works, but I find the narrative of Acts more intelligible and more convincing than do most of those scholars I have named. Luke is not infallible, but he is a generally dependable guide.

Floyd V. Filson

CONTENTS

I

The Book of Acts: Scope, Purpose, Impact

For the study of the rise and early development of the Christian church no writing is more important than the book of Acts. Burton Scott Easton once wrote that Acts is "... the most popular historical work the world has ever seen ..."[1] Even if we were to consider this statement a bit too generous, we still can understand Easton's enthusiasm for the book. Two significant facts do much to underline its importance. One is that the book of Acts deals with the three crucial decades at the beginning of the church's history. These earliest decades were decisive for all later church development. The other fact is that we possess no other narrative account of those decisive early years. Whenever we find another history of the rise of the Christian church, as in the fourth-century *Church History* of Eusebius, the later writer always and necessarily bases his work on the book of Acts. It is the one independent narrative available for the study of the history of this formative period of the church.

The title of the book is misleading. The wording of the title usually found is "The Acts of the Apostles." It was not given to the writing by the author, but was added later by scribes who copied the work. Its implication is that the actions of all of the

1. See *Early Christianity: The Purpose of Acts and Other Papers,* edited by Frederick C. Grant (Greenwich: The Seabury Press, 1954), p. 41.

Apostles are here reported. In three respects, however, this title is not accurate.

1. For one thing, the book is interested not only in the deeds but also in the sermons and speeches of the Christian leaders. As reported in summary form in the Acts, these numerous speeches occupy about 20% of the total book. They thus were obviously of great importance in the writer's eyes.

2. It is also noteworthy that the book speaks of the acts of very few of the Apostles. Of the Twelve, apart from Peter, we hear only of the death of Judas, the election of Matthias, the fact that John went with Peter on two occasions, and the death of John's brother James. In plain words, Peter is the only one of the Twelve who acts or speaks in a definite and individual way in this history of the apostolic church. A few of the others, as noted, are mentioned in passing; most are not mentioned at all outside of the bare listing of their names in Acts 1:13.

3. The traditional title of the book of Acts has another drawback. Such a title may suggest that this is an entirely independent writing. It is impossible, however, to understand Acts rightly unless we keep constantly in mind its close tie with the Gospel of Luke. As Henry J. Cadbury has emphasized in his book, *The Making of Luke-Acts,* the Gospel of Luke and the book of Acts really constitute one two-part work. It was common practice in ancient historical writing to break the total work into parts. The work opened with a preface to the entire history, as is done in Luke 1:1-4. Then, at the beginning of the second (and any further) part the author referred back to what he had already written, just as is done in Acts 1:1. We will misread the history of Acts if we do not keep this in mind. It may be that some time elapsed between the completion of the Gospel of Luke and the writing of the Acts. However, it could hardly have been a long time, and when the writer, who in my judgment was "Luke the beloved physician" (Col. 4:14), wrote what we call the book of Acts, he was clearly conscious that he was continuing and completing the project he had begun when he composed the Gospel of Luke.

CONTENTS AND SCOPE

Before we consider the purpose and impact of the book of Acts, it is important to observe the contents and scope of the work. This will give a clue to the writer's aim. It also will help to explain his influence on the church. There is admittedly no general agreement on the outline to be found in the writing, and it is by no means certain that Luke carefully formulated an outline before he began to write. Nevertheless, it will be instructive to consider what outline best brings out what the book means to say.

Some scholars have taken Acts 1:8 as Luke's outline: "But you shall receive power when the Holy Spirit has come upon you; and you shall be my witnesses in Jerusalem and in all Judea and Samaria and to the end of the earth." This verse is indeed significant. It calls clearly to our attention these basic facts: The book tells of the work of the Spirit in the Apostles and the church; the work of the Spirit is not primarily emotional thrill but rather power for Christian life and witness; the mission of the Apostles and the church is to witness to Jesus Christ; and this witness is to be given to the entire world. But this does not give us an outline. It is true that the narrative begins in Jerusalem, as this verse indicates, but contrary to the order in this verse we hear next of preaching in Samaria before we find mention of preaching in Judea, and the reference to "the end of the earth" provides no outline at all of the step-by-step expansion that follows the preaching in Samaria and Judea. Acts 1:8 does not give us an outline of the book.

Others would oversimplify that problem by dividing Acts into two parts. In the earlier part, Peter is dominant; in the latter one, Paul holds the center of the stage. This calls attention to basic facts, but it is not an adequate outline.

Of the possible outlines suggested, by far the most instructive seems to be the six-panel division which C. H. Turner proposed.[2]

2. See his article "Chronology of the New Testament" in *A Dictionary of the Bible,* edited by James Hastings, Vol. I (New York: Charles Scribner's Sons, 1905), p. 421.

He found six divisions or panels, each of which concludes with a summary statement of the progress of the gospel:

1. Acts 1:1—6:7 tells of the church at Jerusalem under the leadership of Peter and the rest of the Twelve; Barnabas is introduced briefly. The summary in 6:7 reads:

> And the word of God increased; and the number of the disciples multiplied greatly in Jerusalem, and a great many of the priests were obedient to the faith.

2. Acts 6:8—9:31 takes up the story of the Greek-speaking Jewish Christians and recounts their ministry in Jerusalem, Samaria, the coastal plain of Palestine, and Damascus. Attention returns to Jerusalem at the close of the section, which tells of the choice of the Seven and of the work of Stephen, Philip, and Saul. The summary verse, 9:31, reads:

> So the church throughout all Judea and Galilee and Samaria had peace and was built up; and walking in the fear of the Lord and in the comfort of the Holy Spirit it was multiplied.

(This is the only time that the book of Acts mentions Christians in Galilee.)

3. Acts 9:32—12:24 recounts the spread of the church to Phoenicia, Cyprus, and Antioch in Syria. Here as in the preceding section attention returns to Jerusalem in the closing portion. The leading figures are Peter, Barnabas, and Saul; James the brother of Jesus is merely mentioned, but in a way that suggests his growing prominence. The brief summary sentence in 12:24 reads:

> But the word of God grew and multiplied.

4. Acts 12:25—16:5 tells first how Barnabas and Saul go from Jerusalem to Antioch, whence they are sent out on a mission which reaches Cyprus and southern and central Asia Minor. Peter and James the brother of Jesus are prominent in the conference at Jerusalem which considers the basis on which Gentiles may enter and live in the church. The summary verse, 16:5, comes after the agreement reached at the Jerusalem conference has been reported to the churches previously founded; it reads as follows:

> So the churches were strengthened in the faith, and they increased in numbers daily.

5. Acts 16:6—19:20 shows Paul as the one prominent figure; Silas, Timothy, Aquila and Priscilla, and Apollos play quite minor roles; this is the period of the independent Pauline mission to Macedonia and Achaia and to parts of Asia Minor, especially Ephesus. Again the summary verse, 19:20, is quite brief:

> So the word of the Lord grew and prevailed mightily.

6. The sixth and final section, Acts 19:21—28:31, is by far the longest of the six; it includes nine and a half chapters. To this striking fact we must return. The section opens with Paul's decision to visit Jerusalem and then go to Rome; it tells of his final visit to churches already founded, of his voyage to Jerusalem, and then, after his arrest in Jerusalem and long imprisonment at Caesarea, of his voyage to Rome. It closes with Paul in prison in Rome but free to preach to all who come to him. Acts 28:30-31, the summary sentence and conclusion of the book, reads as follows:

> And he lived there two whole years at his own expense, and welcomed all who came to him, preaching the kingdom of God and teaching about the Lord Jesus Christ quite openly and unhindered.

This outline is useful and on the whole faithful to the content of Acts. It leads us to make certain comments:

1. First of all, it must be admitted that neither this outline nor any other gives proper expression to the important role of the sermon summaries and speeches in the total book. The successive speeches show no progressive development of the Christian message and so give no basis for an outline. But they are important in any serious study of the book of Acts.

2. Noteworthy is the fact that the church, inspired and directed by the Holy Spirit, had the power to persist in its Christian witness and make steady progress in spite of continual opposition and persecution.

3. An exceedingly important aspect of the story is the geographical expansion of the church.

4. The key role of the Jerusalem church is obvious; the story starts in Jerusalem and keeps returning there until Paul's final departure for Rome.

5. The movement of the story is on the whole toward Rome. The gospel does not move south to Egypt or east to Mesopotamia; rather, it takes the road north and west until it finally reaches Rome, which thus is regarded as the terminal point of the story.

6. As already noted, the main focus is on two leaders, Peter and Paul. For Luke, no other early Christian leader can compare with them in importance.

7. It is remarkable, however, that most of the leaders in the history are not numbered among the Twelve. If we ask what persons take an active and influential role, there are six who stand out. This "big six" includes Peter, Barnabas, Stephen, Philip, Paul, and James the brother of Jesus. Only one of these six was a member of the Twelve.

8. Paul's final journey to Jerusalem and the resulting voyage to Rome must have had immense importance in Luke's eyes. If we assume, as we must, that the way a writer closes his book is significant, and that the amount of space he gives to a section reflects its importance, this long closing section of Acts demands special attention. One-third of the entire book is used to tell the story of this journey. Paul's mission work was obviously of outstanding significance for Luke, but this final journey takes up more space in Acts than does all the other travel and work of Paul. On the ground of space used it might even seem—though I would hesitate to go so far—that this final journey was more important to Luke than was all of Paul's mission preaching. The emphasis on this journey, therefore, calls for study and explanation.

For fear that what has been said may suggest that Acts gives a complete picture of the origin and development of the apostolic church, it may be well to note briefly certain striking limitations in its content:

1. It does not cover the entire New Testament period. In fact,

most of the New Testament books were written after the end of Paul's two-year imprisonment in Rome. Thus Acts does not provide us with the setting in which to place their writing.

2. Even in the time period covered, the story leaves great gaps. We are not told when or how the gospel first reached Rome. Some geographical areas are ignored completely. If Christianity extended to Egypt in this period, we hear nothing of it. If the gospel was carried to Mesopotamia, that step is not reported. If in these three decades preachers took the Christian message to northern Asia Minor, Acts gives us no clue as to when this occurred or who went there.

3. Even in the places where Acts tells us that churches were planted, we are told almost nothing about the inner life and development of those churches. We know, for example, that Paul worked in Corinth and that he visited the church there more than once, but Acts tells us nothing of the internal problems of that church which we know so well from 1 and 2 Corinthians. What Acts tells us is rather how the gospel came to a city, how the messengers won their first converts, and in most cases how the missionaries came to preach not only to the Jews but also to the Gentiles, and then how Paul came to leave that place. The book does not give us a study of the internal life of the individual churches; it gives us rather a picture of the expansion of the church.

THE PURPOSE OF THE AUTHOR

After the foregoing survey of the contents and scope of the book of Acts, we are ready to ask what the contents reveal of Luke's purpose in writing this narrative. To obtain a true answer to this question, we must keep in mind the fact that Acts continues the story told in the Gospel of Luke. This directs our attention to the literary preface which opens that Gospel.

The very presence of that preface and the other marks of literary concern and competence show a literary aim; Luke wanted to write a work which would command respect among cultured people. This is a new note in the Gospels; the other canonical Gospels show no such concern. It is possible also that the dedication to Theophilus (Luke 1:3; cf. Acts 1:1) reflects an ambition to gain the attention and response of people in high official or social circles. We cannot determine with certainty whether Theophilus was a Roman official, as may well be the case, or was rather a patron or friend prominent in social circles and interested in learning more of the Christian faith. It is barely possible that the word "Theophilus" does not refer to a man of political or social station but is merely a symbolic name; it literally means "God-lover" or "friend-of-God" and conceivably could refer to any Christian or serious inquirer. But the expression "most excellent" probably indicates a person of high station, and the address to such a person indicates Luke's conscious literary stance.

But more important than Luke's literary aim was his intention to write history. Modern historians would undoubtedly approach the task differently, but, as Cadbury has shown, numerous parallels demonstrate that Luke used methods followed by other historical writers of his era, and it is clear that in his view the most effective way to achieve his purpose was to tell the story of the life and work of Jesus and the rise of the church. In Acts his aim was to tell the story of the rise and spread of the church from its earliest days in Jerusalem to its authoritative establishment by Paul in Rome.

The full sweep of Luke's total narrative constituted a revolution in Christian writing. Paul had written letters. Others had written more or less complete gospel accounts (cf. Luke 1:1). But when Luke came to write the basic Christian story, he saw that the Christian gospel message could not be adequately or truly presented simply by writing a Gospel. It took both the Gospel and the story of the emergence of the church to tell the basic Christian story. To know and understand the gospel one must know both the Gospel story and also the story of the apostolic church and its apostolic witness. This basic gospel message was in its essential nature a special kind of history: It could only be grasped as a story; it included both the Gospel story of Jesus' career and the story of the apostolic church. Luke's purpose was to write in its full sweep the most important history that could be told.

Thus the purpose of Luke was a Christian purpose. His concern for literary form was meant to serve the spread of the gospel. His interest in history was demanded by the very nature of the gospel, which is the story of God's saving work begun in Christ and then given authentic witness through the Apostles inspired by the Holy Spirit.

The dedication to Theophilus must not mislead us into thinking that Luke wrote only to win "eggheads." That idea must be rejected in view of at least two considerations. For one thing, Luke aimed to win a much wider range of people than the intellectual or social elite. The popular style, on which Easton comments, shows that the writer was concerned with speaking to common folk who can follow a vivid narrative with interest and response. A second point which demands notice is that Luke wanted to inform and confirm and strengthen the faith of Christians who would hear this story of their church read to them in Christian gatherings. The attempt to reach into intellectual circles marks a new accent in Christian writing. But it was not the sole or even the dominant note in Luke's work. He aimed at a much wider public. He aimed to help his fellow Christians and to win all who would listen to his story.

Thus Luke's main purpose was positive. He told the story of the preaching and the spread of the gospel in order to confirm faith and win new believers in the Roman world. But it must also be noted that he had secondary, apologetic motives for writing Luke-Acts. Such apologetic interest comes out in both the narrative and the speeches. It can be seen in three ways:

1. Luke frequently and emphatically insists that Christianity is the true Judaism. To be sure, he frankly reports that official Jewish leaders continually opposed the Christian preachers, especially Paul. He makes it clear that in the overwhelming majority of conflicts it was the Jews who started and provoked opposition to the church. But he never tires of pointing out how wrong and unjustified such Jewish opposition was. His Gospel starts and ends in the Temple at Jerusalem. The church had its formal

beginning in Jerusalem, and it never gave up that center until the perverse opposition of official Jewry forced it to do so. Both the life and the work of Jesus, and the stages of development in the apostolic church, fulfill God's promises found in the Old Testament. The Christian leaders were loyal to the ancestral faith; even Paul could honestly claim that. It was the supreme mistake of history for the Jews to reject Jesus their Christ and turn their backs on the apostolic gospel.

Their mistake meant that the church was now the true Israel. Because of its roots in the Old Testament, its continuity with the Old Testament faith, and its continued loyalty to the true faith which official Jewry wrongly disowned, the church could rightly ask Rome, as Luke does in Luke-Acts, to grant to the church all the official recognition and protection which she was in the habit of granting to Judaism. Against the charges of Jews that the gospel was a new message and a perversion of Judaism, Luke stoutly asserted that the gospel embodied the fulfillment of God's promises to Israel; it was those who believed the gospel and witnessed to it who were the true Israel.

For Luke this was a critical issue. Such a crucial question can only be answered fully by the decision of faith, but Luke tried to make his demonstration convincing enough to the public and especially to the Romans so that even if not converted they would at least regard the Christian faith as the continuation of Judaism and therefore entitled to all the respect and protection that the Romans had already agreed that Judaism should receive. Luke held, as Easton said, that ". . . Christianity, and Christianity alone, is the true Judaism."[3] This is an apologetic statement, but it is also a positive statement: that in its essential nature Christianity roots in the Old Testament, is continuous with the Old Testament people of God, and is now the true heir of God's promises to that people.

2. Luke repeatedly brings out the fact that Christianity is not politically dangerous. It does not aim at political revolution. This, however, was not so easy to prove as we tend to assume. For

3. *Op. cit.*, p. 47.

us, the church and the Christian faith are so very respectable. But Jesus had been condemned to death as a political rebel by Pilate; that was the meaning of the title "the King of the Jews" when it was nailed to the cross (Luke 23:38 and parallels). Later Christians have seen irony in that title, since Pilate wrote more truly than he knew. But that was not Pilate's intent; he condemned Jesus, sincerely or in pretense, as a rebel against Rome. The Apostles, especially Peter and Paul, were arrested repeatedly on suspicion of disturbing the peace or making revolutionary plots. But Luke can say truly that both the Herodians and Pilate in the days of Jesus, and the Roman governors and soldiers of the Apostolic Age, considered the claim and program of the Christian group and found nothing subversive in it. He can cite a long list of vindicating decisions, from Pilate's threefold statement that he found no fault in Jesus (Luke 23:4, 14-15, 22) to the repeated statement that Paul had done nothing to justify indictment or condemnation (Acts 23:29; 25:25; 26:31).

Considering the outwardly unfavorable situation, Luke did remarkably well. He did not deny the record—he could not. But he vindicated his heroes by citing a succession of official pronouncements of innocence; he intended thereby to win sympathy and remove the prejudice that would keep people from hearing and receiving the Christian message.

3. A more personal apologetic purpose is found in the powerful defense which Luke makes of the Apostle Paul. To us Protestants Paul is a hero. We praise him even when we do not fully understand him. His preaching to the Gentiles as well as to Jews, and the defense his letters make of the truth and universality of the gospel, impress us so deeply that we often fail to see how hounded and hated he was, and how often men misunderstood and misrepresented his gospel.

The Jews regarded Paul as a renegade; did he not take Gentiles into the church without requiring them to keep the Law? As Acts indicates, they followed him from city to city and worked incessantly to undermine his influence among Jews of the Dispersion.

The Gentiles and, in particular, the Romans were indifferent to his theological departure from the official "party line" of the Judaism of his day. But his untiring work to win not only Jews but especially Gentiles to his faith could only succeed at the cost of disrupting the polytheistic, pagan, morally lax way of life of most Gentiles. Moreover, Paul always preached with an intense urgency which made him violently critical of the *status quo* and stirred excited response in those who believed. To many observers all this made him seem a professional troublemaker who ought to be driven out or shut up in prison so that people could have peace. What many lethargic Protestants think about Holy Rollers and excitable Pentecostal sects resembles to some extent what the average Gentile thought of such men as Paul. The difference is that whereas we share a common biblical message with modern emotional sects, the Gentiles, including the Roman officials, had no such common ground with Paul, and did not welcome his indictment of their Gentile way of life.

There is still more to say. The Christians started out with an eschatological message for which the permanent duration of the *status quo* was neither assured nor desired. Early Christian preaching contained, at least implicitly, an inherent criticism of both society and government, just as all faithful Christian preaching does today. That criticism probably found some rather startling apocalyptic expressions at times.

Luke is cool to such alarming apocalyptic expressions of the eschatological hope. His apologetic concern may be one factor in his less eager expectation of the imminent end of this world. He accepts the Roman world and government as likely to endure longer than some of his fellow Christians, including Paul, had thought. And for that lengthened interim period he maintains that the church is not a political threat. The Christians are worthy of respect and protection by the Empire.

Paul in particular was under continual attack by Jews and others as a dangerous and subversive character. It was Luke's deep concern to show Paul's innocence. This may be a large part of the purpose of the long section of nine and a half chapters with which Acts closes. One after another, military men and governors recognized and stated Paul's innocence. It was important to Luke to make that point. He thought it important for the standing of the church in the Empire for Paul to have that vindication.

Indeed, Luke was right. Jews, Christians, and pagans of the Empire attacked Paul. Had he been permanently discredited, the future of Christianity would have been different from what it was. But in fact the book of Acts became canonical, and in harmony with Luke's aim Paul was accepted as the great missionary and theologian of the church. This meant that the gospel of grace, the universality of the gospel, and the ethical integrity of Spirit-led life in faith were protected in a way which otherwise would have been impossible. The apologetic of Luke on behalf of Paul was of crucial importance for the future understanding of the gospel and for the future life of the church.

THE THEOLOGY OF LUKE

Because the history told in Acts is the history of a religious movement and was written with a Christian purpose, it is important to note the main features of the writer's Christian thought. These features emerge mainly in the "sermons" and speeches, and they do much to clarify the writer's purpose and explain the impact of his work.

It must be conceded frankly, however, that these speeches are at best but meager summaries of what was said on the occasions indicated. To imagine that Peter and Paul preached two-, three-, or five-minute sermons would be a great mistake; Paul could argue all day (Acts 28:23), and he could preach all evening until midnight and then, after seeing to Eutychus, continue to converse until daybreak (Acts 20:7-11).

Not only are these sermons summaries at best, but they are also in the style of Luke himself. He either gave literary form to what he was informed the various speakers had said, or else he composed speeches containing what he thought each speaker might have said on that particular occasion. It seems to me that while Luke is responsible for the literary form and for some of the thinking back of these speeches, he usually had traditions or personal memories which enabled him to give to each report an authentic note which suited the speaker and the occasion. He was not concerned, however, with accenting differences between various preachers. He knew that the various leaders differed somewhat in the way they stated the gospel, but he was convinced that in essentials they all preached the same gospel, and he saw no real clash between them. As is clear from variation in details in the three accounts of Paul's conversion, he was not bothered by minor differences (cf. Acts 9:1-19; 22:3-16; 26:9-18). He sensed, and aimed to reflect, a fundamental agreement among the preachers reported.

This indifference to minor variations is one hint of the fact that Luke was not a vigorous and systematic theologian. But like every other Christian who uses the mind God gave him, Luke had a theology, and it is worthwhile to try to state it. The very writing of the book of Acts reflects a theological point of the greatest importance. Luke realized that the apostolic witness to Jesus Christ was an essential part of the good news which the church was to take into all the world. The witness to Christ's death, Resurrection, exaltation, Lordship, and gift of the Spirit was an integral part of the gospel. It was the special task of the Apostles, who included more leaders than the Twelve, to give that witness. As time passed, the written record of that apostolic witness was needed, and when the voices of the original Apostles were all stilled, that written record inevitably assumed basic and permanent importance for the church. As far as we know, it was Luke who saw most clearly this basic theological fact of the essential role of the apostolic witness and took care that the church should not lose that witness from view.

If we ask where we can best begin to state in more detail the theology of Luke, the book of Acts strongly suggests that we begin with the central importance of the Resurrection of Jesus, his ascension or exaltation to the right hand of God, his gift of the Holy Spirit to his followers, and the constant power and guidance and joy which the Spirit gave to the church. This will not mean that Luke neglected the life and teaching of Jesus. On that point we shall say more later. The writer of Acts had already written the Gospel of Luke, and he had in mind all that his

Gospel contained; he thought that all he reported in that Gospel was basic and immensely important. But as we study the preaching in Acts we find that the Resurrection and its sequel are the focus of attention; they shape the thinking of the writer and the apostolic church. Even the tactful and cautious approach to the Athenians comes to a climax in the witness to the Resurrection (Acts 17:31).

The mention of the speech in Athens raises a question. Did Luke think that there was one gospel for the Jews and another for the Gentiles? This can hardly be granted. Luke himself was evidently a Gentile. He took it for granted that the Old Testament was his Scripture, that the history of Israel was the background of his Christian faith, that the promises of God in Scripture had been fulfilled in Jesus Christ, and that all Christians should unite in grateful acceptance of these facts. How then are we to explain the fact that the "sermons" to pagans at Lystra and Athens are so different from the "sermons" to Jews in the earlier chapters of Acts? At Lystra (Acts 14:15-17) and Athens (Acts 17:22-31) Paul says almost nothing about what we consider the characteristic Christian message.

It may help here if we recall that Cornelius and his household were Gentiles, and that the words of Peter in Acts 10:34-43 include all of the essential features in the "sermons" of Peter and Paul to Jewish groups. It may be replied that Cornelius was already a synagogue-related God-fearer and knew much of the Jewish heritage, which the Gentile Luke himself may have known before his conversion. But this is the very point; as Christians, the Gentiles Cornelius and Luke shared with their Jewish fellow Christians the one gospel, and there is no reason to think that they would have expected other Gentiles to accept only a very limited part of the total Christian confession and theology.

The approach to Gentiles who knew nothing of the Jewish or the Christian faith had to be different from the approach which could be made to Jews or to synagogue-related Gentiles. In dealing with Gentiles unacquainted with Judaism, polytheism and idolatry had first to be opposed; faith in the one true God, the Creator of all, had to be presented; the Resurrection and the judgment had to be attested; and the necessity of repentance, which was first of all the turning from pagan views and ways of life, had to be insisted on. We must not think that Luke (or Paul) thought that this was all that a Gentile needed to do. But it was the way to start; it had to be made clear that the message about Jesus was not just an addition to the already possessed polytheistic world view of these Gentiles; only against a monotheistic background could the distinctive Christian message then be preached and understood. The gospel which centered in Jesus Christ meant a radical break with the pagan world.

But the gospel also meant a radical break with the existing Jewish world. For Luke and for the apostolic church generally, the gospel was, of course, the true Jewish faith. It was based on the Old Testament, whose promises it fulfilled. The God of Israel "brought to Israel a Savior, Jesus, as he promised" (Acts 13:23). In the history of Israel that God could be seen at work, and that history found its goal and climax in Jesus Christ, Israel's "Lord and Christ" (Acts 2:36). The gospel could be grounded in Scripture passages which give the background and the support for every aspect of Christian preaching. But for all the continuity between the Old Testament and the gospel, between Israel and the church, there is a break. The Judaism of the days of Jesus and Peter and Paul was not so smooth a point of connection with the gospel as we might think. The Christians appealed from the views of existing Judaism and its official representatives to the guidance they found in the Old Testament Scripture and its history.

One way in which this break appears is in the historical surveys in the speeches of Acts. They do not carry the story down through the Old Testament times to connect the gospel directly with first-century Judaism. Quite the contrary. They go back to the story of Abraham, Moses, or David, with a brief mention of Solomon, but from those outstanding figures of Old Testament history they leap forward to the story of Jesus and the church. Those of us who see truth in the approach called

Heilsgeschichte, "salvation history," had better take note of this amazing leap of a thousand years or more in the speeches of Acts. Obviously it was not Luke's idea that the gospel's connection with the Old Testament Scripture and history was a smooth, direct, evolutionary tie. The newness of the gospel and its offense to Jews as well as to Gentiles are protected in Luke's way of presenting the apostolic history. The mission and work of Jesus Christ are not just a supplement to the Old Testament story. In the mind of Luke it is clear that the person and work of Jesus were gloriously unique and decisive for his day and for the years to follow.

There is in Acts less emphasis on the saving benefit of Jesus' death than some Christians suppose. The idea is not totally absent either in the Gospel of Luke or in Acts, but it is not so prominent as other aspects of Christ's work. Jesus is the prophet whom Moses promised that God would send (Deut. 18:15-18), and his words and acts are authoritative. He is the Servant of God (Acts 8:32-33), but there is little emphasis on his vicarious suffering. He is the Messiah of Israel; he is the risen and exalted Lord (Acts 2:36). He will come to judge all men (Acts 10:42). But there is no clear and prominent doctrine of the Atonement in Acts. The death of Jesus was necessary in the divine plan. It led to the Resurrection and the exaltation and the gift of the Spirit. But there is no such doctrine of the Atonement as Paul presents in his letters.

The death, the Resurrection, the exaltation, and the gift of the Spirit have introduced a new situation. The gift of the Spirit had been promised for the last days (Joel 2:28-32); now that the promised Spirit has been given, the church is living "in the last days" (Acts 2:17), and through the Spirit it lives with a new power, guidance, and joy. The miracles are an integral part of the new situation and of the Christian witness. The joy in fellowship and the winning of ever more converts are likewise the inevitable results of the presence and the working of the Spirit.

We may call this picture of the new age of the Spirit a partly realized eschatology. But that could be misleading. Luke has no overpowering sense that the end of the age, the end of "the last days," is very near, and he gives one a feeling that the mission of the church to preach the gospel "to the end of the earth" (Acts 1:8) may continue for some time before the end. His writing ends with Paul preaching the gospel in Rome (Acts 28:30-31); this is a symbol that the outreach of the gospel is universal and that the church must reach out to include all peoples of all regions. In other words, the book of Acts ends with an implicit promise of an extensive further program. This is not a note of apocalyptic urgency. It is a note of readiness to accept and carry out the will of God in an ongoing universal mission. The Jews have had urgent and repeated opportunity to hear and respond to the gospel in faith. To me Paul's word in Acts 28:28 that "this salvation of God has been sent to the Gentiles" does not mean that preaching to the Jews will now stop. But the emphasis in further mission work is to be on an enlarging mission to the Gentiles.

The church, which is one church for all believers, is to carry forward what Paul is doing at the end of Acts. It is to announce the sure coming in full and final form of the Kingdom of God; it is to teach men about the Lord Jesus Christ, who, in a way that does not compromise the monotheism of the gospel, is the focal center of the faith, worship, obedience, hope, and witness of the church.

THE ROLE OF ACTS IN THE CANON

In addition to our survey of the contents and scope, the purpose, and the theology of Acts, it is worthwhile to underline the book's decisive role in the New Testament canon. It was the only history of the Apostolic Age, the only narrative expression of the fact that the apostolic witness is an integral and indispensable part of the essential gospel message. Of the use of the book down to the middle of the second century we have no clear report. It would appear that, while it was written in order to form with the Gospel of Luke one historical account of the origin and emergence of the church, it was soon separated from the Gospel of Luke, which was grouped with other Gospels to form the basic four-Gospel collection. This separation might have seemed to doom Acts to a permanently minor or unimportant role. But the final result proved to be the very reverse of this. The church knew of the work and witness of certain Apostles. It had letters from Paul, and by the end of the first century they had been gathered into a collection for convenient use by those churches which looked to him as their founder or Christian spokesman. It had other apostolic writings, though not as many as Paul had left. But it needed one book to bind the apostolic writings together in forceful unity.

It is not entirely clear whether the church had clearly conceived the necessity of a New Testament canon before Marcion, about A.D. 140, formed his own canon. He rejected the Old Testament, and after deleting from the Gospel of Luke and ten of Paul's letters the passages which he thought Jewish-minded Christians had added to them, he used those eleven writings as the total canon of Scripture for his churches. My own conviction is that by the fifth decade of the second century, when Marcion's canon appeared and challenged the rest of the church, the church was already clearly moving toward a New Testament canon. The necessity of such a canon was clarified and made more urgent by Marcion's move.

The church countered Marcion's move by enlarging his conception of the needed canon. It kept the Old Testament. Instead of one Gospel, it accepted four. Instead of the letters of one Apostle, it accepted a larger group of letters, which gave the apostolic witness of both Paul and other Apostles. It added, though more hesitantly and somewhat later, the book of Revelation to its group of authoritative writings. The book of Acts provided the link that joined into one whole the two parts of the canon, the Gospels and the Letters. Acts had a link with the Gospel of Luke that tied it back to the four-Gospel collection. It carried forward the history to recount the beginnings of the church and report the apostolic witness. By making clear this basic function of the Apostles, it made fitting the inclusion of the Letters in the New Testament canon.

If we were not so used to the presence of the Letters in the canon, it would astound us that all but five of the New Testament books are in the form of letters or epistles. Their presence becomes easier to understand, and the New Testament has unity, because the book of Acts gives these Letters a background and a link with the Gospels. With Acts the Letters as well as the Gospels give us the apostolic witness, and their presence in the canon appears natural and secure.

Thus the book of Acts, taken by itself, is our one and indispensable account of the three most crucial decades in the history of the church. It embodies the apostolic witness to Jesus Christ. It reminds us that the Gospels are really a part of that basic apostolic witness. It links the story of the ministry and earthly work of Jesus with the narrative of how the original apostolic witness widened its outreach to accept the world as its field. It gives the ground for the inclusion of the Letters in the New Testament canon. It recognizes and uses the Old Testament as Scripture while it also recognizes and underlines the decisive and unique work of Jesus Christ and the radical importance of the apostolic witness to him. It thus has immense importance in the formation of the canon and in all later understanding of the meaning of Scripture.

Few writings have made so great an impact on human history. The book of Acts was written with the sound conviction that the gospel can only be rightly understood by telling the special history of God's dealings with men through the history of Israel, the coming of Christ, and the proclaiming of the apostolic witness from Jerusalem to Rome. The book has proved of immense importance for the formation of the canon, for the later building and guidance of the church, and for the continual shaping of Christian theology. The author undoubtedly had theological limitations, and a prominent part of his purpose was to write history and give it an attractive literary form. But it must be said to his credit that his book has had a rare and impressive theological impact.

II

Preaching and Teaching in the Apostolic Church

The speeches of Acts occupy about one-fifth of the total extent of the book. This clearly indicates that they were of great importance to Luke and so deserve special attention in a study of the early years of the apostolic church. Indeed, they have played a prominent role in leading books on New Testament study. If we are asked what are the three most influential books of the last two generations of New Testament and theological study, we would have to list first Karl Barth's commentary on *The Letter to the Romans;* no other book can match its impact on biblical and theological study in the years since World War I.[1] The second outstanding book which I would mention is C. H. Dodd's *The Apostolic Preaching and Its Developments.*[2] The third is Rudolf Bultmann's relatively short but highly provocative essay on "New Testament and Mythology."[3] It is Dodd and Bultmann, more than any others, who have set the pattern for the current discussion of the preaching of the apostolic church.

1. The first German edition appeared in 1918, the rewritten second edition in 1921. (English translation, London: Oxford University Press, 1933.)

2. Published by Hodder & Stoughton in 1936. I use the American edition (New York: Harper & Brothers, 1962), by permission.

3. This essay, first published in 1941, was included in Vol. I of *Kerygma und Mythos,* edited by H. W. Bartsch (1951). R. H. Fuller translated this volume, *Kerygma and Myth* (London: S. P. C. K., 1953).

KERYGMA AND DIDACHE

The book by Dodd deals directly with the question of the preaching of the earliest church, and it is worthwhile to recall the essentials of his presentation. Determinative for all of his discussion is the basic distinction he makes between *kerygma* and *didache* ("preaching" and "teaching"). By "preaching" Dodd means ". . . the public proclamation of Christianity to the non-Christian world" (p. 7). The Greek word *kerygma* refers to the gospel message which the Apostles preached to make converts. To put it another way, it is the evangelistic message that aims directly and urgently to win unbelievers to put their faith in Jesus Christ. Dodd rightly notes that most of what we call "preaching" today is not preaching by this standard but is rather teaching, exhortation, or discussion of the application of the gospel to various aspects of Christian thought and practice.

The description which Dodd gives of *didache* or "teaching" is not so satisfactory. He defines it as ". . . in a large majority of cases ethical instruction. . . . [but] Occasionally . . . the reasoned commendation of Christianity to persons interested but not yet convinced. . . . [and] Sometimes . . . the exposition of theological doctrine" (p. 7). It is clear that for Dodd *kerygma* and *didache* are two quite distinct things.

THE EARLIEST PREACHING MESSAGE

The question then arises as to where we can find a trustworthy record of the original evangelistic message. Dodd finds two ways to reconstruct it. One is to examine the Letters of Paul. As they stand, of course, they are not a transcript of the *kerygma*. But embedded in them are traditional statements, whose very wording and almost liturgical style show that Paul did not formulate them but took them over from the earliest preachers. Using these fragments, Dodd assembles the affirmations which were essential in the earliest apostolic preaching. This is his summary (p. 18) of the Pauline *kerygma:*

The prophecies are fulfilled, and the new Age is inaugurated by the coming of Christ.

He was born of the seed of David.

He died according to the Scriptures, to deliver us out of the present evil age.

He was buried.

He rose on the third day according to the Scriptures.

He is exalted at the right hand of God, as Son of God and Lord of quick and dead.

He will come again as Judge and Saviour of men.

Paul's gospel message may have contained more, but it certainly contained these points. Note how important Paul's testimony is. It takes us back to within a very few years of the death of Jesus. It gives us in a very early form the apostolic message which he heard from the church and shared with other early preachers.

The other way Dodd finds to get back to the earliest preaching is to study the "sermons" of Acts. He does not claim that they are authentic transcripts of the very sermons preached on the occasions indicated in Acts, but his study of their language and content satisfies him that the "sermons" in Acts 2-4 report with substantial accuracy what was preached in the earliest Jerusalem church. He makes a special study of these "sermons," and he also uses both Peter's "sermon" in the household of the synagogue-related Gentile Cornelius at Caesarea (Acts 10:34-43) and Paul's "sermon" in the synagogue at Pisidian Antioch (Acts 13:16-41). From Acts 2-4, Dodd gets ". . . a comprehensive view of the content of the early *kerygma*. . . . summarized as follows: . . . the age of fulfilment has dawned. . . . this has taken place through the ministry, death, and resurrection of Jesus . . ."; here is included "His Davidic descent. . . . His ministry. . . . His death. . . . His resurrection. . . . by virtue of the resurrection, Jesus has been exalted at the right hand of God, as Messianic head of the new Israel. . . . the Holy Spirit in the Church is the sign of Christ's present power and glory. . . . the Messianic Age will shortly reach its consummation in the return of Christ. . . . the *kerygma* always closes with an appeal for repentance, the offer of forgiveness and of the Holy Spirit, and the promise of 'Salvation,' that is, of 'the life of the Age to Come,' to those who enter the elect community" (pp. 21-23). Thus, Dodd continues, ". . . what the author of Acts meant by 'preaching the Kingdom of God.' . . . follows the lines of the summary of the preaching of Jesus as given in Mark [1:14-15]: 'Jesus came into Galilee preaching the Gospel of God, and saying, "The time is fulfilled, and the Kingdom of God has drawn near: repent and believe the Gospel"'" (p. 24). While the Jerusalem *kerygma* and the Pauline *kerygma* are not identical, they are largely in agreement, and we may take it as assured that we know fairly well the early evangelistic message of the apostolic church.

It is Dodd's conviction that the developments in the New Testament message moved out from this basic gospel. The Gospels have individual features, but ". . . the fourfold Gospel taken as a whole is an expression of the original apostolic Preaching." These Gospels ". . . embody the original apostolic Preaching of the 'saving facts' . . ." (p. 55). Paul, as has been stated, is loyal to the basic *kerygma,* but in his Letters there is a ". . . transformation of eschatology into 'mysticism' . . ." (p. 64), by which ". . . full justice is done for the first time to the principle of 'realized eschatology' which is vital to the whole *kerygma*" (p. 65). The Fourth Evangelist gives a ". . . profound restatement of the apostolic Preaching . . ." (p. 73); he succeeds in ". . . subordinating the 'futurist' element in the eschatology of the early Church to the 'realized eschatology' which . . . was from the first the distinctive and controlling factor in the *kerygma*" (p. 66).

It would be wrong to think that Dodd worked out this statement in isolation from other New Testament scholars. There had been other expressions of deep discontent with the earlier liberal picture of Jesus. Dodd set the seal on the reaction against the liberal "Jesus of History"; he made it crystal clear that the church from the first preached a gospel of salvation which embodied a high Christology. He provided an effective statement of the fact that the various writings of the New Testament give converging expression to the same basic gospel.

Only those who lived through the generation immediately following the First World War can appreciate the difference in climate between the nineteen-twenties and the years since the publication of Dodd's book in 1936. Whatever we may feel compelled to say in criticism of his views, we are essentially on his side in his presentation of what the gospel message was in the first decades of the church.

TWO CRITICISMS OF DODD'S RECONSTRUCTION

This extensive agreement with Dodd does not bar criticism and correction of some aspects of his position. First of all, it is a question whether it makes for concreteness and clarity to import the Greek word *kerygma* into English and use it for the content of the earliest evangelistic message. The word means nothing to most Christians and in itself carries no explicit meaning.

What is essential for us is not to lose from sight just what it was that the writer of Acts says of the content of the preaching. That message dealt with "the kingdom of God" (Acts 19:8; 28:31); it dealt with the decisive acts by which God was establishing his effective rule in accord with his promise and his gracious will. It could be called "the word of God" or "the word of the Lord" (Acts 12:24; 19:20); it was a message which told of the saving acts of God through Christ, and though spoken by chosen men it came from God, centered in Christ, and was preached under the guidance and power of the Spirit. It could be called "the gospel" (Acts 14:21; 16:10); it was the good news of God's saving acts preached to men who desperately needed forgiveness, new life, and power. Because the message was so frankly Christocentric, it could be indicated simply by referring to "Jesus as the Christ" or "the Lord Jesus Christ" (Acts 5:42; 28:31); through Jesus, the promised Messiah, ministering on earth, crucified, raised, exalted, and destined to come to judge all men, God acts to provide a gospel for the world. Because the Resurrection is so central and significant in the apostolic message, it could be indicated effectively by the words "Jesus and the resurrection" (Acts 17:18).

These expressions used in Acts for the content of the early

Christian preaching may of course be used in thoughtless and superficial ways. But they have a direct reference to the message and work of Jesus, to the divine source of the message, to the glad note which such a redemptive message contains, to the basic confession of Jesus as "Lord and Christ," and to the central significance of the Resurrection in apostolic faith and preaching. It is hardly an improvement to introduce an esoteric word which Acts never uses and make that word the algebraic *x* which vaguely points to the gospel.

A second criticism worth noting is that Dodd's distinction between preaching and teaching is not supported by Acts. The two words are not sharply separated in New Testament usage. Undoubtedly there is a difference between the way one presents the gospel to non-Christians in an urgent appeal for acceptance and conversion and the way one by teaching explains and defends and applies the Christian message in dealing with inquirers and believers. But it is not possible to divide the content of the total Christian message and use a basic part for preaching and the rest for teaching. The preacher is always free to use any aspect of Christian truth that will give him an attentive and responsive hearing. The teacher must use all his skill to make the total Christian message clear, persuasive, and relevant. Both use the same essential content, and the same man may preach at one time and pass over to teaching without a break or hesitation.

We read of Jesus that he taught and preached. This does not mean that he compartmentalized his ministry so that sometimes he taught, and on other occasions he preached, but never did anything that could be called both teaching and preaching. He certainly presented his one message in various ways. He had the urgency of an evangelist; he had the patience and the will to explain which teaching requires. At one time one approach would dominate, and at another time the other approach would control his method; but it was one message and the two approaches could not be kept completely apart (cf. Matt. 4:23; 9:35; Luke 20:1). The same thing was true in the Apostolic Age, if Acts is any clue. The way "teaching and preaching" are coupled shows this (Acts

5:42; 15:35). So does the linking of teaching and proclaiming (Acts 4:2). When Paul "preached" Jesus and the Resurrection, the Athenians are said to have called it a "new teaching" (Acts 17:18-19). "Preaching the kingdom of God and teaching about the Lord Jesus Christ" are not two completely separate activities (Acts 28:31). Even if in later days of church history some men were evangelists and others were teachers, in the New Testament the same person was often found doing both. Such was the case with Jesus and the Apostles.

THE ROLE OF THE WITNESS

The debate over the relative importance and possibly different function of preachers and teachers may divert attention from the fact that in the book of Acts the presentation of the Christian message receives a unity through the use of another term to describe the role of the Apostles. "But you shall receive power when the Holy Spirit has come upon you; and you shall be my witnesses in Jerusalem and in all Judea and Samaria and to the end of the earth" (Acts 1:8). The words "witness" and "testify" occur some thirty-five times in the book of Acts. This impressive total means that the preaching and the teaching by the Apostles are ways of making their witness effective.

The Greek word for witness is *martys.* An alternate ancient form of the word, identical with the stem still in use in the New Testament period, is *martyr.* The later use of the word, the use familiar to modern Christians, was to refer to one who gave his witness to his faith or cause by suffering and usually dying for it. This use, however, is rarely if ever found in the New Testament. Even in Acts 22:20, where the death of Stephen is in mind, it is probably the witness of Stephen in word and faithful life that is meant when he is called the witness of Jesus. The interest of Acts is in the witness of Christian preaching and teaching. The accent on witnessing by a good and faithful life is still a minor theme, and the idea of witnessing by suffering or death had not yet become the normal meaning of the word *martys.*

In the book of Acts the verb *martyreō,* "to witness," refers to personal testimony to the content, truth, and urgency of the gospel message. The witness is a person who is in a position to know the things of which he speaks and so can attest their truth. He is a person whose testimony is needed by others if they are to know that truth and accept it. In the human situation not all people have direct access to the facts on every important issue. It is a quite common necessity to have to rely on trustworthy witnesses in order to know what happened and so get the basis for understanding the event's meaning. We live in a world where we are continually shut up to this dependence on others for useful and sometimes crucial information. We, of course, have to accept the testimony by our own decision. We cannot escape that personal responsibility. We must accept it and let it have its effective place in our life. In this act of acceptance and of use we are personally involved; we respond to the truth, and thus we understand the situation which the witness makes it possible for us to face.

The witness to the gospel message in the book of Acts was testimony to the actual occurrence of events. It included also interpretation of what God was doing in those events and what meaning those events had for the hearers of the testimony. This involvement with God's saving work explains the fact that the witness is variously said to be that of God himself (Acts 15:8), of the Holy Spirit (Acts 5:32; 20:23), or of the prophets (Acts 10:43). One way by which God bore witness was through the signs and wonders which he did through the Apostles Paul and Barnabas (Acts 14:3). But the usual New Testament way of speaking of witness refers to the verbal witness which men give to God's acts.

It is interesting and significant to note who is said to give this witness in Acts. Only one is not called an Apostle. This is Stephen. Because of his stirring courage in word and faithful life he is called, in the words of Paul to the Lord Christ, "thy witness" (Acts 22:20).

Apart from this one special case, it is only the Apostles who are called witnesses. Paul and Barnabas are included in this group; they are rarely called Apostles in Acts (14:4, 14), but it is they and the Twelve who give the basic witness to the gospel. It is obvious how Paul can be included in the core group of witnesses (and some similar explanation may be assumed for Barnabas). It is because the risen Christ had appeared to Paul and called him to a special ministry. Paul could not testify at firsthand, as could the Twelve, to the events and teaching of Jesus' public ministry. It is noteworthy that while Dodd finds some evidence that the public ministry was included in the outline of the apostolic preaching as given in "sermons" of Peter, he finds no such evidence in the Letters of Paul.

This helps us realize the importance of the Twelve in the early years of the church. Even though they individually—except for Peter—are not vocal in Acts, they as a group have a unique connection with the public ministry of Jesus and an unmatched background knowledge of his doings and teaching. Their testimony covered the full range of the ministry, from the baptism of John the Baptist to the Resurrection and the exaltation of Jesus (Acts 1:21-22).

In the case of Paul it was only the Resurrection to which he could give the same direct testimony as the Twelve. But in the book of Acts this witness to the Resurrection is the key witness, and so we understand how Paul can be considered so nearly on a par with the Twelve in his witness; he as well as they could witness to the Resurrection. This central role of the witness to the Resurrection finds striking expression in Acts 1:22; the candidates nominated to take the place of Judas Iscariot must have firsthand knowledge of the entire ministry of Jesus, but the actual function of the one chosen is to join the Eleven and "become with us a witness to his resurrection."

We are so indoctrinated with the central importance of the death of Jesus that it is hard for us to realize that this was not the accent of the Apostolic Age. The Resurrection was central; even the death of Jesus was seen and interpreted in the light of the Resurrection. The basic witness of the Apostles was to the Resurrection of Jesus. They had seen the risen Christ; they could testify with complete confidence that he had risen from the dead.

HISTORICAL EVENTS ATTESTED IN CHRISTIAN WITNESS

This theme of witness enables us to put the preaching of Acts in proper perspective. The hearer of the preaching is confronted by a message and a witness. He should accept the message; he should believe in Jesus Christ. But he does this by recognizing in the preaching witness a trustworthy guide and friend. The response to the message is bound up with the attitude toward the human witness. I emphasize this point because there is a tendency in our day to ignore it.

Rudolf Bultmann in particular has stressed the existential position in a way that gives no adequate place to the witness we are studying. For Bultmann the *kerygma* is a bare statement of the facts of God's redemptive action and offer. The hearer is confronted by this bare declaration. He is not to argue or discuss the *kerygma*. God confronts him in this message, and his part is to respond in an act of decision that accepts the offered grace of God in Christ.

There is something true and vital in this view. We do not believe the gospel simply because it is in the Bible, or because the church says it is true, or because intensive historical study convinces us that such faith is reasonable and justified. We respond to God, confronting us in the *kerygma*. We act in the responsible present; we respond as persons who sense that this story concerns us; it is our situation to which the *kerygma* speaks, and before God we individually decide in faith and in obedience.

But in the post-Bultmannian era, as it has too pretentiously been called, it has been widely realized that we must affirm a solid historical content in that basic gospel message. In fact, the existential gospel message affirms such a content. No emphasis on the existential involvement of the hearer can be allowed to obscure that historical basis of the message. The immediate validity of the message and the historicity of the basic story are both essential and interlocked.

One thing more must be said. It is the point to which the foregoing discussion of witness leads. The faith of us later

Christians rests upon the witness of others. The existentialist may be troubled by this fact, but that dependence is inescapable. We depend on the apostolic witness. The role of the Apostles and the permanent necessity of the New Testament as the deposit of that basic apostolic witness are here involved. From the point of view of Acts and from the point of view of Christian theology it is not sufficient to say that we each independently face God's claim and make our response in the ever-new present.

We are indeed existentially involved; we are confronted by God's claim in the gospel; it is not the Apostles or the church or the Bible or our mothers or our pastors who can answer for us; we cannot be Christians by living on the merits of the faith and obedience of others; we cannot even live on the basis of our own past decisions to believe and obey. These are some of Bultmann's insights which we must welcome and cherish.

But we are rooted in history; the factual basis of the gospel message is indispensable; the interpretation of the decisive events of the gospel story must never obscure the fact that the gospel depends on the historicity of those central events; the trustworthy testimony which apostolic witnesses give to those events and their meaning is an essential factor in our Christian position; in the wisdom of God we are tied to the witness of the Apostles; and our faith is never possible without hearing the apostolic witness and accepting it as trustworthy. The apostolic preaching is a witness, and the human witness as well as his words are permanent factors in the Christian situation in which we live and worship.

THE APPROACH TO PAGAN GENTILES

There is one other general observation about the apostolic preaching before we turn to study the teaching of the apostolic church. Dodd's aim was to get back to the earliest form of preaching to be found in the New Testament. For that purpose he used Peter's sermons in Acts 2-4 and supplemented them by Peter's "sermon" to Cornelius and his household (Acts 10:34-43), with some reference to Paul's "sermon" in the synagogue in

Pisidian Antioch (Acts 13:16-41). In other words, he used sermons said to be preached either to Jews in Jerusalem and in the Dispersion, or to a group of Gentiles closely linked with the synagogue. He left out of account such personal defenses as the amazingly militant speech of Stephen (Acts 7:2-53) or the largely biographical speeches of Paul before the various Roman rulers and officers (Acts 22-26). Neither was he concerned with reconstructing the method and content of evangelistic preaching to pagans who had no connection with the synagogue. Gentiles such as Cornelius, who had been in touch with the synagogue, had a background knowledge of Scripture and the history of Israel; they were committed to monotheism, elevated worship, and high moral standards. They knew of God's promises to Israel. They could hear with understanding the gospel story of the fulfillment of those promises in Jesus Christ. But to preach to polytheistic, idolatrous, and morally lax pagans was another matter. What did the Christian preachers say to them? In view of the great interest of the Gentile Luke in the Apostle Paul, we might expect Acts to give a great deal of information on this question. In the present study of the apostolic witness we need to look again at this issue.

Only two passages in Acts offer direct testimony as to how the gospel was preached to complete pagans. One is the horrified protest of Paul and Barnabas when preparations were being made to offer sacrifice to them at Lystra (Acts 14:15-17); it does not profess to be a full-scale presentation of the gospel. The other is the famous address of Paul to the Athenians on the Areopagus (Acts 17:22-31).

As is well known, there is a widespread critical view that these are not trustworthy reports of what was said on the occasions described. Certainly their wording is Luke's own composition.

But two things deserve to be said. One is that the approach of these two "sermons" is quite like that of Jewish attempts to speak to pagan Gentiles on behalf of the Jewish faith. In a world of polytheism and idolatry it was necessary to present the basic message of monotheism, the one God who is Creator, Lord, and

Judge, and under whom all life is lived. It was necessary to state clearly man's moral responsibility before God, and in doing this the Resurrection and the final judgment were proclaimed. It was urgent to call pagans to repentance, which in this situation meant to turn to God before judgment came. This was the necessary background for appreciating the specific content of the Jewish Scripture, worship, and way of life.

Similarly in Christian preaching it was necessary to present God as the one God, the Creator and Judge, before preaching the distinctive gospel. To interest a polytheist in Jesus might merely increase by one the number of that pagan's gods; it would not necessarily make him a monotheistic believer in God and a true disciple of Jesus Christ. Whether such an approach—by beginning with monotheism—was the only possible one may be debated; it is at least a fact that this actually was the way Jews went at the job of winning a hearing from pagans, it was at least one way that early Christian preachers must have used, and it seems to me inevitable. Luke's two "sermons" to pagan Gentiles fit into the general situation of the Apostolic Age.

The other thing to be said about these two addresses to Gentiles is that they are not to be understood as presenting all that Luke wanted Gentiles to believe. It is clear throughout the Gentile mission in Acts that faith in the Lord Jesus Christ is the objective of the apostolic preaching. The words of Paul and Barnabas at Lystra are brief and obviously not the complete gospel. The address at Athens is often thought to be a fragment; it is said that the Athenians interrupted Paul just when he was ready to launch into the specific Christian content of his message. I doubt this, for at the end Paul speaks of the Resurrection and the final judgment. But this view contains an element of truth: that Luke does not mean what he presents to be the entire content of what Paul had to say to pagans.

The basic conclusion which I gather from these two speeches is that Luke knew quite well that Christian preachers to pagans were using and had used in earlier years an approach which first cleared away polytheistic and idolatrous views and so prepared pagans to see the real meaning of the gospel. For Luke, for Paul, and for the apostolic preachers generally, the Old Testament was Scripture; it contained a promise fulfilled in Jesus Christ; the church was the true Israel; Jesus Christ crucified and risen was Lord and Christ; the Holy Spirit was given to believers; Jesus would judge all men; and all who accepted in faith and dedication the good news of God's saving acts shared the confident expectation of God's care and blessing now and in the time to come. I have the impression that in Acts Luke does not mean to tell for every city the complete content of Paul's preaching and the details of that local church's life. He often singles out one special incident and is content to tell of it, and it would be a fatal mistake to conclude that he intended to present that one event as the complete ministry of Paul in that particular city. He aimed at variety and rapid movement in his narrative. In earlier chapters of Acts he had presented the basic gospel message enough times to make clear its essential content. He adds two scenes from Paul's preaching to pagans to show special aspects of the approach to them. These aspects must be supplemented by a look at the earlier "sermons" of Acts.

TEACHING IN THE APOSTOLIC CHURCH

We turn now from a study of the basic content of the evangelistic preaching of Acts to consider the teaching that was carried on in the apostolic church. It has already been emphasized that there is no sharp separation between preaching and teaching. The basic content is the same; the teaching will include the basic gospel message, though it will deal more with the understanding and the living of the Christian life in the light of that basic gospel. The people addressed by the preaching and the teaching are also much the same group. The basic evangelistic message was no doubt heard in gatherings of Christians as well as in missionary sermons, and the teaching process went on in the work of winning new converts as well as in the task of training Christians, especially recently converted Christians, to live the Christian life. The aim in both preaching and teaching was first to win men to an initial response of faith and obedience and then to build up all believers in a better understanding of God's grace and a more complete obedience to God's will.

Four comments may be made on the place of teaching in the apostolic church. First of all, there is frequent mention in Acts of the teaching activity of both the Twelve and the Apostle Paul. It is clear that they preached, but it is equally clear from the frequent references in Acts that they continually taught. "The apostles' teaching" was a regular feature in the Jerusalem church (Acts 2:42). Saul (Paul) was one of the "prophets and teachers" in the church at Antioch (Acts 13:1), and he in his Letters and Luke in Acts make it clear that he carried on teaching in his churches. We have no right to belittle teaching by thinking that the great leaders left it to subordinates while they themselves concentrated on preaching alone.

A second comment may seem of minor importance, but it tells us a great deal about the method and the message of the teaching work of the church. It is interesting to note that Stephen, and especially Paul, "disputed" and "argued" in the synagogues (Acts 6:9; 17:2; 18:4, 19). The picture is one of lengthy discussions in which the gospel was submitted to intensive examination by opponents and to extensive and earnest development by Stephen and Paul. The implication seems clear that the correspondence of the gospel with Scripture and with Jewish hopes was examined in detail. Such passages make it plain that Paul met with much stubborn opposition in the synagogues and that he persisted in his teaching as long as he could get a hearing. Most of these synagogue debates and discussions seem to have been on the Sabbath and to have been connected with the weekly service on that day; the all-day discussion at Rome (Acts 28:23) was a special occasion. But the series of references indicates that extended teaching and discussion was common practice. Moreover, the fact that Paul "argued . . . in the market place every day" at Athens, and "argued daily in the hall of Tyrannus" at Ephesus, and "argued" in extended discussion with Felix (Acts 17:17; 19:9; 24:25), shows that it was not only with Jews that he held extended arguments and presented his message in detail. This was teaching, but such intensive Scripture study and earnest debates were also one form of evangelistic activity.

It is important—this is a third comment—to consider the meaning of the fact that the so-called "sermons" in Acts are at best only summaries of what Luke thought the preachers said. These compact statements of the gospel message could give the false impression that those early preachers shunned illustrations in their sermons. They could make it seem that the preachers stated a bare outline of strict essentials and were promptly done. I wonder if it is the brevity of these summaries that is largely or partly responsible for the impression Bultmann gives that the *kerygma* is to be announced but not supported by argument or detail, and then the answer is to be given without argument, study, discussion, or question, once the hearer has thus been confronted by God in the *kerygma*. I have always felt that a word should be said on behalf of those hearers who wanted a bit more detail and felt entitled to have an answer to some questions before making a decision.

The truth is that those apostolic preachers never rushed through a two- or five-minute sermon and then called for decision. Take Paul. He could argue all day with Jewish leaders (Acts 28:23); he could talk until Eutychus fell out of a window, and then, shortly after the interruption, resume and go on until dawn (Acts 20:7-11). These men had a great deal to say in support of their basic topics. What are called the "sermons" of Acts must be thought of as the barest outlines of the preaching message. The actual presentation of these points required expansion to clarify, explain, illustrate, and enforce them. The speaker had to answer the demand for information; he had to answer the objections which arose in the minds of his hearers.

In other words, preaching, in the actual expanded form in which it occurred, included a great deal of what we think of as teaching. For the unbeliever this teaching was necessary to clear away haziness, ignorance, questions, and objections. For the believer it was necessary to give a clearer understanding of the basic gospel message which he had already accepted but did not fully understand or know how to apply. Once it is seen that the so-called "sermons" are very meager summaries of the preaching message, we are free to say that abundant and varied detail would enter into the actual process of preaching. The sharp distinction between *kerygma* and *didache* becomes less marked once this simple truth is seen and its implications are recognized.

GOSPEL TRADITION IN APOSTOLIC TEACHING

Our fourth comment concerns the role of tradition about the ministry, teaching, death, and Resurrection of Jesus in the teaching work of the Christian leaders. Dodd thinks that the teaching activity of these leaders involved mainly ethical instruction but also included the reasoned commendation of Christianity and the exposition of theological doctrine. The fact that in this description he omits teaching as to what Jesus did and said is the more puzzling in view of his statement that the Gospels on the whole faithfully reflect the preaching message of the early church. It is not clear why he gives no prominent or explicit place to gospel tradition when he defines the teaching activities of apostolic Christianity. The matter deserves discussion.

The issue as to the preservation and use of the gospel tradition about Jesus has come up in various forms at successive stages of gospel study. When two Apostles (Matthew and John) were thought to have written Gospels, and two disciples of Apostles (Mark and Luke) were credited with the authorship of the other two Gospels, the matter was simple. Apostolic memory, put in writing directly or through a trustworthy disciple, guaranteed the authenticity of the material. It was particularly noted that Papias told how Peter in his ministry habitually used the gospel material, including both the words and the deeds of Jesus.[4] The Apostle used the material in teaching as occasion suggested; the final writing down of the material by Mark gave a written record of material continually used by Peter.

4. See the quotation from Papias in Eusebius, *Church History*, III.39.15.

When theories of written sources back of our Synoptic Gospels, or at least back of Matthew and Luke, came into vogue, they, too, assumed the continual use of the gospel tradition in the life of the church. Whoever wrote down the material of Q, for example, was recording sayings (and a small amount of narrative) which had been used especially in the teaching work of the church, and he did so in order to provide a teaching help for other teachers in the church. (This did not preclude the use of the document in worship.) The hypothesis that written collections of Scripture passages were made and used in the teaching work of Christian leaders was another aspect of the view that written teaching aids were used in the writing of at least Matthew and Luke, and possibly of Mark and John.

When, following the First World War, the method of gospel study known as "form criticism" came into use, much less emphasis was placed on written sources back of our Gospels. Such sources were still assumed to have existed and to have been used in writing our Gospels. But the great emphasis was directed to the earlier, oral use of the gospel tradition in the worship, the teaching, and the controversies of the church. This method of study has generally been connected with extremely negative results as far as the dependability of the Gospels is concerned. But there is no inherent reason why this should be so. The method does assume that the church's needs guided the preservation and use of the gospel material as well as the shaping of the individual units of tradition; the focal concern was not the scholarly writing of accurate history but the formulating of tradition in a way that would be most helpful for the life of the church. Such an approach need not have the hostile theological presuppositions that have often controlled it. The critical scholarly world is gradually feeling its way back to more solid ground after a period in which it was widely axiomatic that we can know nothing definite about the historical Jesus. Günther Bornkamm[5] and James M. Robinson,[6] for example, now speak

5. In English translation, *Jesus of Nazareth* (New York: Harper & Row, 1960).
6. *A New Quest of the Historical Jesus* (London: SCM Press, 1959).

on this subject in somewhat more positive terms than was the case with some earlier scholars, and Robinson insists that Bultmann always did have a more positive note in his gospel criticism than was usually realized.

The position that the gospel material was preserved in connection with the life and the needs of the church, and that its separate units were shaped and continually used in that setting, permits the conclusion that the church knew the historical aspect of its message to be essential and that it was successful, as Dodd maintains, in keeping clear and usable the essential facts about Jesus' life and teaching.

The book of Acts tells little of this. It does refer in 2:42 to "the apostles' teaching." It keeps mentioning teaching by the Apostles. It is hard to believe that such teaching ignored the facts about the ministry, teaching, death, and Resurrection of Jesus.

In this connection it will be worthwhile to note again an often neglected fact. The writer of Acts (Luke) had already written the Gospel of Luke. Few scholars have denied that statement, and there is no good reason to deny it. But if he had already written the Gospel of Luke, this fact teaches us a great deal. The reader of Acts may be tempted to assume that Luke had no interest in the deeds and the words of the historical Jesus. The summary accounts of the apostolic preaching do not use incidents from his life as illustrations. With the exception of one saying, "It is more blessed to give than to receive" (Acts 20:35), Acts never quotes a saying of Jesus from his public ministry. This taken by itself could raise the question of whether the writer of Acts knew the gospel tradition, or whether, if he knew it, he considered it of any importance. In view of the idea that the apostolic church had little interest in the historical Jesus, it is well worth while to raise and answer these questions.

The answer must take account of at least three facts:

1. The writer of Acts certainly knew the gospel tradition, for he had already written the Gospel of Luke. He knew all of the tradition he had there recorded, and he probably knew still other traditions which he had no room or motive to include.

2. He assuredly thought that tradition important, for he had taken the trouble to gather, sift, arrange, and compose in effective form the gospel tradition recorded in the Gospel of Luke. In fact, it is reasonable to assume that he expected the reader of Acts to read the story of the apostolic church with the content of the Gospel of Luke clearly in mind. The fact that he thought it necessary to continue his story to include the apostolic history and witness does not mean that he intended to belittle or neglect the gospel story of Jesus' ministry, death, and Resurrection. His purpose was not narrow but inclusive.

3. But the fact that the "sermons" of Acts do not quote freely the sayings, parables, incidents, and miracles of Jesus' ministry helps us to see the place of the gospel tradition in the church. The framework of that tradition is the gospel message of the saving action of God. It was in fulfillment of God's promises and as the climax of God's work with Israel that Jesus of Nazareth came. He came not merely to give a noble example or to train men by teaching so that they could meet life in their own power, but to save men by his ministry, death, Resurrection, exaltation, continuing Lordship, and final defeat of sin and evil.

The gospel thus is not in its essence the story of a good man, a great teacher, an inspiring example, a noble hero, a steadfast martyr, or a stirring leader, although these aspects of the life and the work of Jesus are included in the total picture. The gospel is rather the story of God's gracious saving action on behalf of sinful men. The historical tradition can be and must be taken up and included in the larger picture of God's plan and redemptive work, but the meaning of the content of Acts, written by a man who knew the gospel tradition and valued it highly, is that the historical facts must fit into the great central affirmation of the gospel of the powerful grace of God. Their role is to contribute to the urgent appeal to men to repent and believe in the Lord Jesus Christ and so receive forgiveness of sins and the gift of the Holy Spirit.

III

Peter and the Twelve

At least two facts prompt a careful study of the role which Peter and the Twelve played in the apostolic church. For one thing, these leaders were the living link between the ministry of Jesus and the early church, and so it is of the utmost importance for historical study to determine as clearly as possible their part in the church's foundation and earliest development. In addition, the current interest in church union directs attention to Peter and the Twelve. In any discussion which deals with differences between denominations and possibilities of church union, the form and leadership of the church in its first years are rightly the object of interest.

THE TWELVE IN THE GOSPELS

We look first at the Twelve as a group. Our concern in these chapters is with the book of Acts, but we cannot discuss the Twelve without briefly recalling the appointment of the Twelve and their relation to Jesus during his ministry. Occasionally it has been questioned whether Jesus actually selected twelve followers and treated them as a separate group who had not only a special relation to him but also a special function. There is no sound basis, however, for such skepticism. The Twelve have a solid place in the gospel tradition. Paul cites a Resurrection tradition from the earliest days of the church to remind the Corinthians that Jesus when risen appeared "to the twelve" (1 Cor. 15:5). And the fact that there was among the Twelve a traitor, Judas Iscariot, is an item whose place in the tradition would be hard to explain if the Twelve were merely a pious invention of the Apostolic Age. It may be taken as fact that Jesus chose the Twelve for a special purpose.

The names of the Twelve require brief attention. We have four lists: Matthew 10:2-4; Mark 3:16-19; Luke 6:14-16; and Acts 1:13 (which has only eleven names, since Judas Iscariot is no longer in the group). There is no list in the Gospel of John, but it definitely refers to Jesus' choice of the Twelve in 6:70. The differences in order in the four lists constitute no serious problem. Simon Peter is always named first. There is some tendency in these lists to group the names in pairs. So with Peter we find Andrew named in Matthew and Luke, while in Acts John is named with Peter, perhaps because in Acts 3:1 ff. and 8:14 ff. Peter and John travel and work together. But, in Mark, James and John are grouped with Peter, to reflect the fact that Peter and James and John formed the inner trio of the Twelve. In any case, the two pairs of brothers, Peter and Andrew, and James and John, always provide the first four names.

The order of the next four names in the list varies for no definable reason. In any case, the four names are Philip and Bartholomew and Matthew and Thomas.

In the last four, James the son of Alphaeus is always named first, and Judas Iscariot is always named last (except that he is not named at all in Acts, since he was then no longer a member of the group). Simon is always included, but his identifying title varies. He is called either "Simon the Cananean" or "Simon the Zealot," but this variation raises no problem, since the title "Cananean" represents an Aramaic word which means "Zealot." As to the identity of the remaining member of the Twelve, however, there is a serious question. In Mark his name is given in most manuscripts as "Thaddaeus," although a minority of manuscripts of less value give the name "Lebbaeus." In Matthew weighty manuscripts support the reading "Thaddaeus," and this may well be the best reading in that Gospel as in Mark, but there is some good evidence in manuscripts of Matthew for the reading "Lebbaeus," and this reading is further supported by the extensive evidence for the reading "Lebbaeus called Thaddeus," in which "Lebbaeus" seems the earlier reading; the variant reading "Thaddeus called Lebbaeus" has very little support. But whether the original text of Matthew agreed with Mark in listing "Thaddaeus" here, or instead read "Lebbaeus," Luke and Acts have still another reading, "Judas the son of James."

The early church was not certain of the name of this one of the Twelve. This is the astonishing conclusion of a study of the four lists, and it is an eloquent testimony to the fact that some of the Twelve were not individually outstanding.

Why did Jesus choose the Twelve? Mark 3:14-15 says that ". . . he appointed twelve, to be with him, and to be sent out to preach and have authority to cast out demons . . ." There is no need to try to improve on this statement, and the Synoptic Gospels record a preaching and healing mission of the Twelve through which Jesus, acting with a sense of eschatological urgency, enlarged the outreach of his itinerant ministry. The Twelve were with him to learn his message and catch his spirit, and they went out to extend his work into areas which he did not have time to visit personally.

At the Last Supper, when Jesus faced imminent death, the Twelve were with him (except that Judas Iscariot left during the supper). Their companionship meant much to him. He spoke with them of the dark days ahead and tried to prepare them to continue his work when he could no longer lead them in the concrete and visible way that had marked his ministry.

THE ELEVEN RALLY AND MATTHIAS IS CHOSEN

And so we come to the role of the Twelve in the book of Acts. At the start they are but eleven, for Judas Iscariot had left them during the Last Supper and shortly thereafter met his death. Just how he died we are not certain, for we have two divergent traditions about it (Matt. 27:3-10; Acts 1:18), but there is no reason to doubt his early death. Rallied by Peter (cf. Luke 22:32; 24:34), to whom the risen Christ appeared (1 Cor. 15:5), the Eleven met the risen Lord. Where they first met him is disputed. In Luke and Acts one is given to understand that it was in Jerusalem and Judea (cf. Luke 24:49; Acts 1:4); the only hint that might point to another answer is that all of the one hundred and twenty persons in the group of disciples gathered in Jerusalem before Pentecost are said to be Galileans (Acts 1:15; 2:7). In Mark the promised scene for the meeting with the risen Christ is Galilee (Mark 14:28; 16:7), but the ending of that Gospel seems to have been lost, and so that Gospel as it stands does not tell the story of the actual meeting. In Matthew, however, which is close to Mark in narrative content, the meeting of Jesus with the Eleven does occur in Galilee (Matt. 28:16-20). In John the original meetings occur in Jerusalem (ch. 20) but there is an added appearance in Galilee (21:1).

On this puzzling question we need not pause longer; if, as I suspect, the original Resurrection appearances were in Galilee, there were also appearances in Jerusalem, and the fact that the church first took clear form in Jerusalem made it simpler to telescope the story and omit any reference to Resurrection appearances in Galilee. Certainly the definite beginnings of the church and the actual ministry of the Twelve were centered in Jerusalem from the days shortly before Pentecost.

The first thing the Eleven did after they had rallied and Jesus had left them was to find a replacement for Judas Iscariot. It is instructive to ask why they did this. It is not enough to say that he was to be a witness to the Resurrection of Jesus (Acts 1:22). This point is interesting as a reminder that there were many others—more than five hundred, according to 1 Corinthians 15:6—who could testify to that event, and at least some of them had been with Jesus during his ministry. But if a special group were to give the key witness to the ministry and the Resurrection of Jesus, it might seem that the Eleven could testify to what he had said and done, and give an adequate witness to the fact of his Resurrection. Why twelve instead of eleven, when the twelfth man must be someone who had not been one of the Twelve during Jesus' ministry?

Two points may throw some light on this question. For one thing, the very act of choosing a replacement for Judas Iscariot shows that the Eleven considered that they had a work to do, a special function to fulfill, and that they must get ready to carry out their task. The importance of the Twelve was not simply that they had been with Jesus and had been of some help to him in the past. Their greater importance was yet to come.

The other point is that the number twelve was bound up with the number of the tribes of Israel. In the minds of Jesus and the Twelve, it appears, the twelve Apostles represented the twelve tribes of Israel (cf. Matt. 19:28; Luke 22:30). They had a mission to Israel. Their message was to deal with the fulfillment of God's promises to Israel. We may say that the story of Acts widens out beyond the limits of the existing Israel. But this was not the way that Jesus, the Twelve, and Luke thought of it. The expanding church, in their view, would always be the true Israel. The number twelve was symbolic of the full purpose of God for all his people.

So to symbolize that full purpose a successor to Judas was necessary. Matthias was chosen in a ceremony in which the actual choice was meant to be left to God (Acts 1:23-26). For Matthias, as far as Acts indicates, it was a brief moment of glory. The New Testament never mentions him again.

THE FOUNDING ROLE OF THE TWELVE

The reconstituted Twelve are regularly called the "Apostles" in Acts. As the root meaning of the Greek word *apostolos* implies, they were "sent" by Jesus and so by God. As "the sent ones" they had a unique role. They were the acknowledged leaders of the church in its very first days at Jerusalem. The only other leaders ever explicitly called "Apostles" in Acts are Paul and Barnabas (14:4, 14), although when Paul in Galatians 1:19 says regarding his first visit to Jerusalem after his conversion: "But I saw none of the other apostles except James the Lord's brother," he apparently indicates that, less than ten years after Jesus' death, James the brother of Jesus had come to be regarded as an Apostle, and the unique prominence which Peter recognizes for James in Acts 12:17 can be interpreted to mean that, in the eyes of the Twelve, James had been recognized as holding apostolic rank. But Luke hesitates to speak of this James as an Apostle, and the rarity with which Paul is called an Apostle in Acts indicates that in Luke's view the founding role of the Twelve was unique and was decisive for the future life of the church.

In this unique ministry we may discern at least two, and possibly three, specific functions. The immediate and central task was to witness to the Resurrection of Jesus (Acts 1:22). Those who had been with him during his ministry, and had been chosen by him to be closest to him and to extend his work, were in the best position to testify with authority that it was really the same Jesus who had appeared to them. They could give the most effective witness to his Resurrection.

Connected with this basic witness was their ability to testify to the spirit, the events, and the teaching of his ministry. It is not said in Acts that this was their function, but Acts 1:21-22 indicates clearly that the background of companionship with Jesus during his ministry was the prerequisite of an effective testimony to his Resurrection, and this implies that they could not speak of the risen Christ without connecting him with the earthly Jesus and his ministry.

The often asserted third ministry of the group of the Twelve is not so clearly their special work. I refer to the mediating of the gift of the Holy Spirit. One clear instance of this is reported. In Samaria the baptism by Philip did not lead to the gift of the Spirit; only when Peter and John came from Jerusalem and prayed for the new believers did they receive that gift (Acts 8:14-17). It should be emphasized, however, that this is the one case of its kind in the entire book of Acts. Usually the time and manner of the gift of the Spirit are not reported at all, and generalizations from one incident are hardly warranted. At Caesarea, Cornelius and his household received the Spirit apart from the expectation of Peter and without his laying on of hands (Acts 10:44). The only time in Acts that an Apostle mediates the gift of the Spirit, apart from the occasion in Samaria, is at Ephesus; there Paul baptizes twelve former disciples of John the Baptist and lays hands on them, and the Holy Spirit comes upon them (Acts 19:1-7). But in this case it is Paul, not the Twelve, who mediates the Spirit, and it was to persons whom Paul himself had just baptized "in the name of the Lord Jesus."

Thus the idea that the Twelve had to mediate the gift of the Holy Spirit rests upon only one incident, and the bulk of the evidence is against it. There was a freedom about the coming and working of the Spirit that some later ecclesiastical theories fail to recognize.

It has been important to make clear that the Twelve were a definite group who had the central role in the founding of the church and whose witness and leadership must not be ignored. In the theology of Acts, as pointed out in our earlier discussion, this apostolic witness is basic, and the inclusion of Acts in the New Testament canon recognizes the correctness of Luke's position. But most of the individual members of the Twelve did not stand out by reason of any personal activity. Their significance was as a group.

Of the Twelve only three play any role in Acts. One of these is James the son of Zebedee. All that we are told of him in Acts is that he was put to death by Herod Agrippa I (Acts 12:2). This implies that he had been an active leader of some prominence, so that Herod's attention was drawn to him and he was singled out for seizure and execution. That this act "pleased the Jews" (Acts 12:3) indicates that the Jewish leaders were hostile to James and regarded him as a threat to Judaism, either because of his zeal in preaching or because he did not seem sufficiently loyal to the Mosaic Law. Another Apostle singled out for mention in Acts is John the brother of James. He plays a quite minor role. All that is said of him is that he went with Peter to the Temple at the time of the healing of the lame man, was arrested and brought before the Sanhedrin, and later was sent with Peter to Samaria (Acts 3:1, 3, 11; 4:13; 8:14). On each of these occasions it is Peter who speaks; John himself says nothing. Thus apart from the mere listing of names in chapter 1, Acts makes individual mention only of the inner trio of the Twelve, and Peter is the only one of the Twelve whose individual leadership and initative are reported.

THE DECREASING ROLE OF THE TWELVE

It is important to note that when James the son of Zebedee was executed by Herod Agrippa I (Acts 12:2) no successor was chosen. At the beginning of the story of Acts it was considered necessary to replace Judas, and so Matthias was chosen to make the number of the Twelve complete. When James was killed, however, no such necessity was felt. We are not told why. We do know that, by the time of the martyrdom of James the son of Zebedee, Peter had begun to travel about in the coastal region of Palestine (Acts 9:32—11:18); we know also that James the brother of Jesus had already emerged as prominent in the leadership in Jerusalem (cf. Gal. 1:19; Acts 12:17), and that elders had already appeared in the leadership of the Jerusalem church (Acts 11:30). The scene was changing. The Twelve for some time had ceased to have the sole leadership in Jerusalem, and they did not all feel obligated to stay at Jerusalem, as they once had done even in the face of persecution (Acts 8:1).

After chapter 12, the book of Acts has little more to say about the Twelve. On Paul's last trip to Jerusalem, they will not even be mentioned as being present in the city (Acts 21:18). Later legends confidently tell us where each one of them went and what he did, but these on the whole are untrustworthy clues. The fact is that the Twelve slip into the shadows and the focus of the story of Acts moves elsewhere. They last act as a group in Jerusalem at the conference about the basis on which Gentiles may be received into the church (Acts 15:1-29). Even on that occasion, as Luke describes it, James the brother of Jesus is the dominant figure and seems to be included among the Apostles, and he and the elders of the Jerusalem church share the responsibility with the members of the Twelve who were present. This is the last mention of the Twelve in Acts. In Acts 18:22, which I take to refer to a visit by Paul to Jerusalem, Paul "went up and greeted the church," but nothing is said as to whether Apostles were present. In Acts 21:18, as has already been noted, only James the brother of Jesus and the elders are present.

The Apostles no longer lead the church in Jerusalem. The days of their decisive role in the leadership of the church are past. That is the clear implication of the story in Acts, and not a word hints or implies that they did anything to arrange for successors.

SIMON PETER: THE "ROCK"

From this general survey of the role of the Apostles in the earliest church we turn to a study of the special role of Peter. His original name was Simon. It was Jesus who gave him the descriptive Aramaic designation *Kepha,* which means "rock." This Aramaic word was transliterated into Greek in the form *Cephas,* and translated into Greek by the word *Petros,* which likewise means "rock" and from which we get the English name "Peter."

When Jesus first gave this title to Peter is hard to decide. Mark 3:16 and Luke 6:14 probably mean that Jesus did this when he chose the Twelve. Matthew 10:2 does not attempt to fix the time, but Matthew 16:18 seems to put it at the time of Peter's Messianic confession. John 1:42, in a passage which ascribes the Messianic confession to Andrew and dates it even before the public ministry of Jesus opens, says that Jesus gave this title to Simon before he left the Jordan region where John the Baptist had baptized Jesus. It would seem more likely that Jesus gave Simon this title at the time of the choice of the Twelve or at the time of Peter's Messianic confession.

Why did Jesus apply this descriptive title to Simon? It has been explained as jest, as fact, and as promise. Some take it as a jest: poor wobbly Simon, lovable, well-intentioned, always intending to do right, but never able to carry out his declared intentions! A rock in declared firm intention but never in action! This is not fair to the man. He was, to say the least, as loyal and steadfast as the rest of the Twelve, and it must also be said that he was the spokesman and spearhead of the group, the most decisive and solid man of them all.

Much is made of Peter's weakness in denying Jesus on the night of his Master's arrest (Mark 14:66-72 and parallels). But at least Peter got close enough to Jesus to get into danger from the soldiers and the other hostile Jews standing in the court of the high priest's house. Most of the Twelve were hiding out in the dark in the region around Jerusalem, but Peter followed Jesus to the high priest's house, and it was his outstanding courage that got him into the danger which caused him to give in to fear at the critical moment. The jest idea is wrong.

But the idea that the word "Peter" simply described a fact is too flattering to Peter. As we have just recalled, he crumpled when danger became acute. He still was not completely made of martyr stuff. So a combination of actual vigor, courage, and loyalty, imperfect though it was, with the promise of a more complete dedication, may be the meaning we best can see in the title. He was the man on whom Jesus was counting to rally and steady the others (Luke 22:31-32).

PETER'S MESSIANIC CONFESSION AND MATTHEW 16:17-19

In speaking of the meaning of the word "Peter" we have already made some reference to the man's role during Jesus' ministry. He was the leader and spokesman of the Twelve, prompt to speak and to act even when what he said or did was not wise or judicious. In particular, he spoke for the group when he voiced the conviction that Jesus was the fulfillment of the Messianic hopes of his people: "You are the Christ" (Mark 8:29). He did not understand what Jesus meant by his guarded acceptance of that title, and so his identification of Jesus as the expected Jewish Messiah was misleading and in a sense incorrect. But his deep personal loyalty to Jesus and his determination to follow and serve his Master made it possible for him to learn from the cruel facts of Jesus' arrest and crucifixion what the mission and the method of the Christ really were.

Protestants are touchy and skittish about the words of Matthew 16:17-19, in which Jesus is said to have called Simon "rock" and given him a unique place in his ongoing movement. They know that Roman Catholics regard the passage as the chief support for their views on apostolic succession, the Roman papacy, and the entire hierarchical system. Actually, none of these three things is mentioned in the passage, and no such ideas are ever expressed elsewhere in the teaching of Jesus. If, as I agree, Jesus at some time in the latter part of his ministry used these words, he was not setting up a fixed form for a hierarchical church but was referring to Peter's key role in establishing the new form of the church or people of God in which Jesus Christ would be the central, magnetic, and controlling figure.

The words of Jesus may be paraphrased as follows: "You are Mr. Rock, and on you as this rock I will build my church, that is, the new form of the people of God, the congregation of Israel, in which I will be the central figure. Just as in the Old Testament kingdom the steward held the keys of the royal establishment and was effective in seeing that the household functioned as it should (Isa. 22:22), so you, Peter, will be the key man in my plan, and your decisions will have authority and divine approval."

I would add that such a promise was conditional and was not given to Peter alone. In Matthew 18:18-20 the same authority and divine approval are promised for the decisions and requests of the disciples as a group and are even assured for any request made by any two or three of the group. This promise that the disciples, or any two of them, will get what they ask is as sweeping a promise as the Gospels contain. The promise to Peter in Matthew 16:19 is not a whit more sweeping than the promises in Matthew 18:18-20. The trouble starts when people try to make the promise to Peter into an ecclesiastical polity. All of these promises are conditional. It is, or should be, understood that divine approval for what Peter and other disciples do depends on whether their action accords with the divine will and purpose. All spiritual promises are conditional on spiritual accord with God's will and plan.

But Jesus really expected Peter to lead his disciples through the trying days ahead. He made this clear in another saying, found in Luke 22:32, in which temporary failure and ultimate key ministry to the entire group of disciples are combined. Satan will sift Peter like wheat; Jesus has prayed for Peter that his faith may not completely fail. When Peter has turned he is to shore up and strengthen his fellow disciples. This key role is what Jesus had in mind for Peter. It is not enough to say that Jesus simply approved the faith of Peter. Jesus' words, of course, referred to Peter as the one who had made his confession of Jesus' Messiahship and expressed his loyalty to Jesus. But it was Peter, and not just an abstract concept or detached confession of faith, who was the object of Jesus' words. The story of Acts will report that Peter justified Jesus' confidence in him.

PETER'S LEADERSHIP IN THE EARLIEST CHURCH

But Peter's key role in the earliest church was not based simply on that confession of Jesus as Messiah. That confession was involved, of course, but the immediate and central path to leadership was Peter's witness to the Resurrection of Jesus. According to the explicit testimony of Paul in 1 Corinthians 15:5, which reports very early Christian tradition, Peter was the first to see the risen Christ, and Luke 24:34 may mean the same thing. It was a scene in which Peter alone met the risen Christ and recognized who he was. Then, when he had turned from doubt and despair to new faith and courage, he was able to rally and strengthen his fellow disciples (Luke 22:32). He stepped into the leading role which made him, humanly speaking, the apostolic founder of the church.

His leadership in that crucial period had at least five aspects: (1) He wanted the Twelve to be ready to act as the leading group of the disciples, so he proposed and induced the entire group to carry through the choice of a successor to Judas Iscariot, and Matthias was chosen (Acts 1:15-26). (2) At Pentecost he became the effective spokesman of the group, preaching the gospel in the light of the Resurrection of Jesus and the gift of the Spirit (Acts 2:14-41). (3) In the Temple he showed that the Spirit had given healing power to the leading disciples of Jesus; "in the name of Jesus Christ of Nazareth" he healed the lame man and preached to the people (Acts 3:1-26). (4) When seized for such acts and words, whose striring nature disturbed the normal calm and routine of Jewish life at the Temple, Peter had the courage to face prison, stand fast before the Sanhedrin, and renew his bold and public confession of Christ (Acts 4:1-22). (5) When deception threatened to drain away the dedication and enthusiastic loyalty of the Christian group, his withering denunciation of Ananias and Sapphira held the church to its central loyalty (Acts 5:1-11).

The plain fact is that in the earliest days of the church, as described in Acts 1-5, Peter was the apostolic rock on which its life was founded. We rightly honor other leaders, such as Paul, but in a real sense every later leader and all of us later Christians are indebted to Peter for his decisive ministry in those crucial and decisive early days.

In what way did Peter understand and preach the faith he professed? It is clear, as Acts 2:36 would indicate, that he considered Jesus to be the risen Lord of the church and the fulfillment of the Jewish Messianic hope. That was common ground among the very early disciples, and it has come to be widely understood in recent years that the confession of Jesus' Lordship was as much an integral part of the earliest church's confession as was the confession of his Messiahship.

Can anything more specific be discerned? Oscar Cullmann has pointed out that only in Acts, chapters 3 and 4, is Jesus called *pais*, "Servant."[1] In these two chapters the term occurs twice in words ascribed to Peter (Acts 3:13, 26) and twice in prayers uttered when Peter is present and may be voicing the prayer of the group (Acts 4:27, 30). Was Peter the first to undertake in a limited way the development of Christian theology? Was he the first disciple to think seriously about how the ministry and suffering of Jesus embodied the spirit and purpose of

1. See Oscar Cullmann, *Peter: Disciple-Apostle-Martyr*. Second Edition (London: SCM Press, 1962), pp. 66-70.

the Servant of God as found in Deutero-Isaiah? Possibly so. The hypothesis, though it cannot be proved, is attractive, and is correct at least insofar as it recognizes in the earliest Christian preachers possibilities of theological development. Paul was not the first Christian to use his mind to understand and state the meaning of the church's faith in Christ.

PETER AND THE MISSION TO GENTILES

It is a difficult task to determine the extent to which Peter disturbed non-Christian Jews and conservative Jewish Christians by his readiness to receive Gentiles into the church. The question is raised by the remarkable words with which Acts 8:1 ends: ". . . they [the church in Jerusalem] were all scattered throughout the region of Judea and Samaria, *except the apostles*" (italics mine).

This amazing statement that every Christian in Jerusalem except the Twelve fled in the face of persecution need not be taken with full literalness. But in any case it raises the question of why the Twelve were not struck by the persecution which forced most of their fellow disciples to flee for their lives. The remark testifies to the courage of the Twelve, but that is not its full meaning. The obvious suggestion is that the persecuting Jews did not see in the Twelve so great a threat to existing Judaism as they saw in the Hellenistic Jewish Christians led by Stephen and the others of the Seven. This would imply that the Twelve were quite conservative, very careful to observe the Jewish Law and ceremonies and to maintain the prerogatives of the Jews. It would not deny the courage of the Twelve, but it would indicate that since the fanatical outburst of persecution did not touch them, the persecutors must have thought them definitely less liberal than the Hellenists. This deduction, it seems to me, contains much truth.

There is good reason, however, not to describe the Twelve in too conservative terms. Certainly Acts does not. If Acts 1:8 reflects to any degree the understanding of the early church, the church knew that its full task was wider than preaching to Jews;

its mission included Samaria and extended to "the end of the earth," that is, to all men. The approval both of Peter's preaching to the Gentile household of Cornelius (Acts 11:1-18) and of the Pauline mission to Gentiles (Acts 15:1-29; cf. Gal. 2:1-10) shows that none of the known leaders of the Jerusalem church wanted to forbid the preaching of the gospel to Gentiles. (The differences probably concerned when and on exactly what terms the gospel should be taken to the Gentile peoples.)

So it is most reasonable to take Acts 8:1 to mean that the comparatively conservative though not reactionary position of the Twelve marked them off from the more liberal Hellenists in the church at Jerusalem, and as a result the fury of the persecutors spent itself largely on the latter group. This is a vivid reminder, however, that the spearhead of the Gentile mission was never in the hands of the Twelve. Their ministry was essentially to Jews, and they were not equipped to head the mission to Gentiles or to carry out the theological pioneering it involved.

It may be hazarded that among the Twelve, Peter was one of those more open to the wider horizon of preaching. He went with John to Samaria and approved the reception of Samaritans into the church (Acts 8:14-25). He fell into a pattern of itineration in coastal Palestine (Acts 9:32-43), and was brought into touch with the synagogue-related Gentile Cornelius and his household (Acts 10:1—11:18). The vision related in Acts 10:9-16 seems to imply that Peter had scruples about going to a Gentile home. But he went, and when the Spirit fell upon the listening Gentiles, he accepted the inference that God had made the crucial decision for him: These Gentiles were truly converted; they should be baptized and considered full members of the church. Acts does not say that the other members of the Twelve rebuked him for this; "the circumcision party," who in Acts 11:1-2 are distinguished from the Apostles, were the ones who objected because he accepted uncircumcised Gentiles as full Christians, but they had to become silent in the face of Peter's story of the divine guidance that determined what he had done.

The suggestion of the series of events in Acts is that at the time of Acts 8:1 Peter was not regarded as a serious threat to current Judaism. But after his experiences in Samaria and Caesarea, it became clear that he was open to a widening of the fellowship of the church in a way that Jewish opponents in Jerusalem actively opposed. The arrest of Peter by Herod Agrippa I (Acts 12:3) no doubt reflects Herod's responsiveness to the growing Jewish hostility to Peter.

In passing, it may be noted that the killing of James the brother of John at this same time (Acts 12:2), and the fact that John went with Peter to Samaria and approved the mission to Samaria (Acts 8:14-25), show that all three of the inner trio of Jesus' disciples were open to this wider outreach of the gospel. The three disciples closest to Jesus during his ministry knew that what was developing was in accord with the spirit and the outlook which they had sensed in Jesus.

By the time of his arrest Peter had become a marked man. Saved from an imprisonment intended to lead to his execution, he briefly visited his fellow disciples in the home of Mary the mother of John Mark and then "went to another place" (Acts 12:17). Jerusalem had become too hostile to permit him to continue a public ministry there, and the basic reason was that he had come to see more clearly than before the place of Gentiles in the church. This does not mean that he broke with the Christian leaders in Jerusalem. He returned and took part in the later conference concerning the place of Gentiles in the church (Acts 15). But henceforth he lived and worked elsewhere. His founding work was completed, except as he continued it in the founding of new Christian churches in other places.

PETER THE LEADING MISSIONARY TO JEWS

According to the report in Acts concerning the Jerusalem conference, Peter defended the preaching of the gospel to the Gentiles and cited his own preaching to the household of Cornelius as the pioneer example (Acts 15:7-11). But it is worth noting that in recording this statement of Peter, Luke is careful not to say that Peter became a full-fledged missionary to the

Gentiles. That role Peter left to others; after preaching to Cornelius, he went back from Caesarea to Jerusalem and continued his relation to the Jewish Jerusalem church. Paul is very explicit on this point. In Galatians 2:7-8 he makes it clear that Peter's work at the time of the conference was as a Jerusalem-oriented missionary to Jews. It was Paul who was the outstanding missionary to the Gentiles.

Where Peter preached on his missionary journeys the book of Acts never tells. He was no longer the active head of the Jerusalem church. That position fell to James the brother of Jesus. When we read in Acts 12:17 that Peter sent word of his situation "to James and to the brethren," we should not take this to mean that Peter thereby appointed James as his successor or representative; Peter was rather recognizing a fact. James already had been moving toward the position of leadership in Jerusalem. Peter had gradually been pulling up his stakes at Jerusalem, and when persecution was directed chiefly at him, he went elsewhere and continued his preaching. Paul tells us that Peter traveled about and took his wife with him at the expense of the churches visited (1 Cor. 9:5). But we do not know where he went.

PETER AT ROME?

The old tradition that Peter went to Rome about A.D. 42, founded the church there, and acted as its bishop or pope for twenty-five years until his martyr death, can no longer be taken seriously. There is no evidence in Acts that he ever went to Rome. If on other grounds we accept it as true that he did go there, the date of that visit must be toward the close of his life. There is no reason to take Acts 12:17 to mean that Peter then went to Rome.

The reference to a Cephas party at Corinth (1 Cor. 1:12) could reflect a visit of Peter to Corinth, as a result of which converts who owed their faith to his preaching or preferred his leadership and understanding of the gospel formed a special party within the Corinthian church. But the partisans of Cephas at Corinth might have received their knowledge and high estimate of Peter from other Christians who visited Corinth and told of Peter's leading place among the Twelve.

It is certain that Peter went to Antioch in Syria (Gal. 2:11), but it is not clear that he stayed there, and the later tradition that he was the first bishop there has no solid basis. The opening address of 1 Peter (1:1) suggests that Peter may have visited the regions of north and central Asia Minor, but it tells us no more.

There is no reason to doubt that Peter traveled widely, but we cannot recover the details or exact scope of those travels. As far as we can discern, Peter concluded his career as a missionary to the Jews in various areas of the Dispersion.

Because the relation of Peter to Rome is of such great interest, it will be worthwhile to comment on the way in which the ending of Acts bears on that question. We know from Paul's Letter to the Romans (1:8-13; 15:22-24) that there had been a strong church in Rome for many years before Paul ever reached the Roman capital. It is clear also from Acts 28:15 that there were Christians in Rome before Paul's arrival. My impression is that Luke considers Paul's apostolic preaching at Rome to be of great importance. From the combined silence and attitude of both Acts and Romans it is hard to believe that Peter had ever been at Rome before Paul arrived there. It was of immense importance to Luke to record that Paul the Apostle had preached the gospel at Rome "quite openly and unhindered" (Acts 28:31). That made the Roman church a truly apostolic church.

What this means is that if any Apostle is to be named as the "founder" of the Roman church it must be Paul. For the writer of Acts, it was Paul's preaching in that church which made it a truly apostolic church. It is not surprising that Dionysius of Corinth, about A.D. 170, says in a letter to the Roman church that Paul, as well as Peter, founded the Roman church;[2] the tradition was gaining power that Peter was the founder, but the inclusion of Paul is striking, and it is justified, at least from the viewpoint of Acts, for whose writer it was Paul's preaching in Rome which really gave the Roman church its apostolic standing.

2. Quoted in Eusebius, *Church History,* II.25.8.

CONCLUSIONS AND INFERENCES

The foregoing study of the role of Peter and the Twelve justifies the following conclusions and inferences:

1. In the book of Acts the Twelve, who are regularly called the Apostles, exercise a unique function, a fundamental role in the earliest beginnings of the church. As a group they give the apostolic witness to the Resurrection and to the gospel message centered in Jesus Christ. They constitute the core and vital center of the earliest Christian community. Peter in particular is the rock upon whose faith, preaching, and active obedience were built the faith, worship, life, and steadfastness of the church.

2. The wide-ranging missionary preaching of Peter to Jews indicates that he was one of the Twelve who could preach not only in his native Aramaic but also, to some extent at least, in the common Greek used in the Graeco-Roman world. The future of the church proved to be in the hands of those who could preach in Greek, and Peter's continuing and widening preaching must have had this necessary linguistic ability.[3]

3. The book of Acts knows nothing of an apostolic succession in the sense of a ministry formally continued from generation to generation in an unbroken line of formal ordinations. The only leaders who seem to have been formally ordained or set apart by the Twelve were the Seven. They were not set apart to be Apostles or bishops or even pastors; they were to carry on relief work in the Jerusalem community, and they had at least *de facto* leadership among the Hellenistic Jewish believers there. And as far as Acts tells, they had no successors. Stephen was martyred. Philip continued long an active ministry, but at last report was living quietly in Caesarea on the Palestinian coast, with no indication that he held any actual office in the church there (Acts 8:40; 21:8). The rest of the Seven are but names. James the brother of Jesus was not ordained by the Twelve to

3. The second-century statement of Papias (quoted in Eusebius, *Church History*, III.39.15), that Mark was Peter's interpreter, may mean that Peter had very limited ability to speak Greek. But his preaching to Cornelius and his travels indicate that he could speak some Greek in addition to his more fluent Aramaic.

succeed or represent them at Jerusalem; he rose to prominence and authority while they were still present and active in Jerusalem, and there is no hint that his prominence and authority resulted from a selection and ordination by the Twelve.

Nowhere do the Twelve ordain successors or arrange for successors. Neither in Acts nor elsewhere in the New Testament is there any clear evidence of formal apostolic succession such as later theories of church polity have often asserted.

4. The Apostle Paul shatters any neat pattern of apostolic succession through the Twelve. He is called an Apostle, though this occurs but seldom (Acts 14:4, 14). But he was not one of the Twelve and was not ordained by the Twelve. Yet the scope of his ministry matches that of the greatest of the Twelve, and the attention given him in Acts not only exceeds that given to all of the Twelve put together but also marks him as the key figure for the future life and witness of the church.

5. This means among other things that there is no basis in Acts (nor does any exist elsewhere in the New Testament) for the papacy. In fact, as we have pointed out, it is Paul alone who gives apostolic standing to the Roman church. In Acts he is the only Apostle who goes to Rome or has any connection with Rome. His coming to Rome and his preaching there give that church its apostolic basis and standing.

The only New Testament hint of Peter's presence in Rome is in 1 Peter 5:13, where "She who is at Babylon" probably means the Roman church; this would support the view that Peter was in Rome at a date later than the end of Acts, but it would not establish that he had permanent residence there or held formal episcopal office in that city.

6. The real picture of the developing life of the apostolic church in Acts is one of freedom led by the Spirit. There was no fixed polity laid down by the twelve Apostles and so planned as to establish a "regular" ministry. There is a variety of leadership, some of it not even described in its origin but only noted when it has reached a stage of development that shows its effectiveness. The role of James the brother of Jesus and the appearance of elders in the Jerusalem church are aspects of leader-

ship which do not spring from a fixed polity but arise in the course of the life of the church to meet needs that made themselves felt.

The theme of Acts is that the Spirit guided the church and its existing leaders to take the steps which enabled the church to express its witness and live a life of loyalty to Christ. There is nothing in Acts to prescribe one specific polity or to forbid a new polity if that would suit better the new needs of a later day. The one thing that Acts would seem to say on this subject is that the Spirit is free to guide men into new ways to witness and work together. It is wrong to try to determine the formal organization of the church on the fallacious assumption that the apostolic church provides us with a prescribed and mandatory pattern.

IV

James and Jewish Christianity

When we speak of Jewish Christianity in this chapter, it is important to make clear what we mean. The phrase might suggest any form of Christianity held and practiced by persons of Jewish origin. In this sense the Twelve, and almost all of the first generation of Christians, were Jewish Christians. So were many of the original converts in the Pauline churches, for Paul's regular practice was to start his work in the synagogues. Thus the nucleus of his churches was made up of Jews and synagogue-related Gentiles.

It is not in this broad sense, however, that we here use the expression "Jewish Christianity." We use it rather to refer to that form of Christian faith and fellowship held by persons of Jewish descent who combined their Christian confession of Jesus as Messiah with a careful keeping of the Mosaic Law. Even if they were willing to concede that Gentiles might live with less concern for that Law, they themselves felt obligated to observe it faithfully. In the book of Acts it is James the brother of Jesus who is the outstanding representative of this point of view. As one of the chief leaders of the apostolic church he deserves careful study.

"THE BROTHERS OF THE LORD"

This James is referred to by Paul as "the Lord's brother" (Gal. 1:19), a designation which distinguishes him from James the son of Zebedee and also from James the son of Alphaeus. He evidently was the oldest of the four "brothers of the Lord" (1 Cor. 9:5); the other three were named Joses and Judas and Simon (Mark 6:3; cf. Matt. 13:55). The Gospels also mention sisters of the Lord, but they are not designated by a formal phrase, nor are they ever named in trustworthy sources. The attention centers on the "brothers of the Lord."

The actual relation of these brothers to Jesus has long been disputed. There are three views on this question, and each derives its name from the name of its chief champion during a heated debate carried on in the church during the latter part of the fourth century.

Helvidius held what would seem to be the natural understanding of the biblical reference. From a study of Matthew 1:25; 13:55-56; Mark 6:3; Luke 2:7; 1 Corinthians 9:5; and Galatians 1:19, the Helvidian view concludes that the brothers of the Lord were children of Joseph and Mary, born in the years following the birth of Jesus.

Epiphanius supported with a highly emotional tone the view that the brothers and the sisters of the Lord were children of Joseph by a former marriage, and so were all older than Jesus. This Epiphanian view, as is shown by the recently discovered Bodmer Papyrus called *The Nativity of Mary,* can be traced back to the middle of the second century.

Jerome boldly denied that the so-called "brothers" were brothers in any family sense. They were not even half-brothers; they were really cousins of Jesus, and so were not the children of either Joseph or Mary. This Hieronymian view, so called from "Hieronymus," the Latin form of Jerome's name, was apparently Jerome's own construction; at least we find no trace of it prior to his own presentation of it.

The views of Epiphanius and Jerome have two advantages in the eyes of many Christians. (1) They both avoid the conclusion, distasteful to great numbers of Christians, that Mary ever had other children besides Jesus. For Mary to have sinful children in addition to being the mother of the sinless Jesus seems to them incongruous and unacceptable. (2) Both of these views also permit the assertion of the perpetual virginity of Mary, an article of faith regarded as indispensable by large numbers of Christians. I must express my own conviction that it was devotional and theological concerns, rather than trustworthy historical evidence, which prompted the development of these views. The Helvidian view seems the natural conclusion to draw from such evidence as the New Testament contains.

"HIS BROTHERS DID NOT BELIEVE IN HIM"

There is clear evidence that during the ministry of Jesus his brothers rejected his message and refused to follow him. Mark 3:31-35 shows plainly that the brothers were in a different group from the disciples of Jesus. Moreover, on that occasion we are startled at the sharp tone with which Jesus completely rejected his family. This is in striking contrast with other passages which express his high valuation of marriage and enjoin in strong words loyalty to parents and family (e.g., Matt. 15:1-5; 19:3-9; Mark 7:9-13; 10:2-12).

Such a contrast finds its full explanation only in the light of Mark 3:21, where "his friends," as the Revised Standard Version translates the Greek, ". . . went out to seize him, for they said, 'He is beside himself.' " Whoever "his friends" are, they think that his zeal in his ministry shows an unbalanced mind; he should be "seized" and withdrawn from public life until he can calm down and become normal and emotionally stable, instead of being so worked up over his religion. But who are these "friends" who think that Jesus has lost his mental balance? The Greek phrase is *hoi par' autou,* which literally means "the ones from beside him." This seems to me to mean his family, and this is confirmed by the fact that in Mark 3:31-35 the family come to Jesus, send for him to come from the crowd to them, and receive an amazingly sharp rejection which goes so far as to deny any real tie with these people who come to him to get him to stop his ministry.

It is understandable that the other Gospels do not include this startling bit of tradition (Mark 3:21), but there is no good reason to doubt that it is an authentic historical report. Its evidence that Jesus' family did not support him during his ministry is confirmed by the explicit statement of John 7:5 that ". . . even his brothers did not believe in him." All this means that none of his brothers was among the Apostles.

THE CONVERSION OF JAMES

It therefore is unexpected and quite puzzling to find that James and the other brothers of the Lord were in the church from the beginning of the Apostolic Age. According to Acts 1:14, not only "Mary the mother of Jesus" but also "his brothers" were members of the Jerusalem church from the earliest days. The key to this development is found in 1 Corinthians 15:7, where Paul, in listing the Resurrection appearances of Jesus, says: "Then he appeared to James . . ." This passage, it is agreed, refers to James the brother of Jesus, and this is supported by the fact that in an extant fragment of the Gospel According to the Hebrews such an appearance is described. The details of that description are doubtless apocryphal, but in its essential content the description confirms the testimony of Paul. It must also be remembered that in 1 Corinthians 15:7 Paul is quoting the very early gospel tradition which he had "received" when he became a Christian.

The Resurrection appearance to James, then, must be accepted as a fact commonly known in the earliest church. It was not the first Resurrection appearance; it followed the appearances to Cephas, to the Twelve, and to "more than five hundred brethren at one time." Some knowledge of these previous appearances and some influence from them on James may have been involved, but we cannot prove this or recapture the specific setting of the appearance to James.

If James was not a disciple of his brother's during Jesus' public ministry, and was converted by the appearance of the risen Christ, his experience was a remarkable parallel to the sequence of events in the life of Paul. The Apostle Paul had been an unbeliever and a persecutor and was converted by an appearance of the risen Christ. Similarly, and at an earlier stage in the story, James had been an unbeliever, had opposed Jesus' ministry, and then by an appearance of the risen Christ had been brought into the company of believers. The confrontation by the risen Christ had an ecclesiastically effective consequence in both cases; it was the fact that he had seen the risen Christ which made each of these men eligible in Christian eyes to be an Apostle.

It may be that the influence of the person and message of Jesus had laid its hold on James before the death of Jesus, so that he was prepared for the decisive experience of meeting the risen Christ. We may, however, say that the Christian witness had similarly had a pre-conversion influence on Paul, and in both cases we must avoid the temptation to think that such conjectures about psychological development really explain what happened.

The essential fact for our present study is that James, who was not a disciple of his brother's during Jesus' public ministry, became through the Resurrection appearance a key witness of the Resurrection, and this fact, coupled with his family tie with Jesus, laid the foundation for the rise of James to a place of influence and power in the church.

PROMINENT MEMBER OF THE JERUSALEM CHURCH

Where James saw the risen Jesus is not stated by the early tradition which Paul hands on. It may well have been in Galilee; the occurrence of Galilean Resurrection appearances is probable on other grounds. The picture of Acts 1:4, according to which the disciples never left Jerusalem in the days between the Crucifixion and Pentecost, is probably a telescoping of the exciting series of events which took place between the death of Jesus and the formation of the congregation of disciples in Jerusalem. But whether James saw the risen Jesus in Galilee or elsewhere, the event took place within a very few weeks after the death of Jesus, and when the disciples rallied in Jerusalem to face their coming responsibility, Mary and the brothers of Jesus took their place in the expectant group, and so James was from the start a member of the apostolic church in Jerusalem.

Of his own pattern of faith and thought we have no early record. He undoubtedly accepted the crucified and risen Jesus as "Lord and Christ" (Acts 2:36). Jesus had not been "beside himself," as James had once thought (Mark 3:21-22), but had been sent by the Father and throughout his ministry had been doing the Father's will.

It must have taken real humility and grace for James to reverse his previous position and accept his own brother as entitled to so high and unique a role. We with pious or romatic imaginations might be inclined to think that the advantage of the family tie would have made it easy for James to become a believer. But the Gospels indicate that the opposite was true. It could well seem incongruous to James that a brother, a childhood companion, should be given such astounding high titles. But this hesitant or unfavorable attitude which James took during Jesus' public ministry yielded to the unrelenting appeal of Jesus which reached its effective climax in the Resurrection appearance. James took his place in the church, not as a leader at first but as one of the members, sharing the faith in Jesus as the Messiah of Israel and the Lord of the disciples.

What happened to James in the first crucial years of the church we are not told. That James was driven from Jerusalem by the persecution which followed the martyrdom of Stephen is possible, but it is not certain, and I strongly doubt it; James was more conservative than the Twelve, who were able to stay (Acts 8:1). We know from Galatians 1:19 that when Paul came to Jerusalem for the first time after his conversion he saw not only Cephas, whom he says he came to see, but also "James the Lord's brother," and while the Greek of that verse may just possibly support another interpretation, it seems rather clear to me that Paul regarded James as already one of the Apostles.

If such was Paul's view, his testimony is highly important,

for it dates from a time less than a decade after the Resurrection of Jesus, and possibly less than five years after that event. In either case, Paul's words indicate the rapid emergence of James as one of the top leaders of the Jerusalem church. When it is recalled that James was not one of the Twelve and that the Twelve were then active in Jerusalem, this rise of James to prominence is a remarkable recognition of his faith, character, and capacity for leadership. Had he lacked such qualities, his relation to Jesus would not have won him such a role. Paul does not report what understanding he reached with James, but he seems to imply that James accepted him as a genuine Christian.

THE LEADER OF THE JERUSALEM CHURCH

The first time that James is mentioned by name in the book of Acts is in 12:17. (The only earlier reference to him in Acts is the mere mention of the brothers of Jesus in 1:14.) Luke has a tantalizing way of introducing persons and situations into his narrative without giving us the background which would explain their role in the story. In Acts 12:17 he refers to James by name for the first time and with no identifying explanation. If we could not turn to the Gospels which name the brothers of Jesus (Matt. 13:55; Mark 6:3), and to Paul's Letters with their references to James and the brothers of the Lord (1 Cor. 9:5; Gal. 1:19; 2:9, 12), we would not know how to identify him. The only negative clue which Luke has given is his reference to the previous martyrdom of James the son of Zebedee (Acts 12:2); he does not explicitly identify the martyr as the son of Zebedee, but we may be sure that it was James the son of Zebedee who was martyred.

From this negative clue, from later mentions of James in the book of Acts, from the Gospels, and from Paul's Letters we can conclude that in Acts 12:17 Peter is sending word to James the brother of Jesus when he says: "Tell this to James and to the brethren."

This does not mean that up to this time James has been just one of the many undistinguished Christians at Jerusalem, and that now for the first time he is singled out to be given special notice and a distinctive task. It means rather, in confirmation of what Galatians 1:19 has taught us, that by this time James has already emerged as a prominent leader in the Jerusalem church, and now that James the son of Zebedee has been martyred and Peter on his release from prison must leave the Jerusalem group of disciples, James is recognized as the one who inevitably will assume the leading role. Since Peter had recently been itinerating in Samaria and the coastal region of Palestine (Acts 9:32—11:18), it is quite likely that James had already been providing continuity of leadership at Jerusalem and so would now naturally become the outstanding leader there. It is assumed, but not stated, that James at once accepted and fulfilled this role.

LEADERSHIP AT THE JERUSALEM CONFERENCE

There are two other passages in Acts where James is mentioned; they are the only two passages in the entire book where he is said to speak and to act. The first time that he is mentioned after 12:17 is in 15:13-21. The passage concerns the conference in Jerusalem. Those present at the conference are identified as "the apostles and the elders, with the whole church" (Acts 15:22).

Peter spoke to recall his preaching to Gentiles in the house of Cornelius, and he stated his conviction that through him God had led the church to receive Gentiles without requiring them to become Jews and keep the Jewish Law (Acts 15:7-11). Then Barnabas and Paul told of their Gentile mission and recounted the miraculous works by which the Holy Spirit had attested the divine approval of their ministry among the Gentiles they had visited (Acts 15:12).

The climax of the discussion was the speech of James, whom Luke seems here to include not as one of the elders but as one of "the apostles" (Acts 15:6, 22). He recalled that Scripture supports the Gentile mission. He then proposed that the conference should not trouble the Gentile believers by insisting that they keep the Law of Moses, but should only tell them to "abstain from the pollutions of idols and from unchastity and from what is strangled and from blood." The Apostles, the elders, and the whole church accepted the solution which James proposed and, through a letter carried by two commissioned messengers, sent their decision to the churches of Antioch, Syria, and Cilicia.

It has sometimes been said that James presided at this famous Jerusalem conference, but in reality the book of Acts does not say who presided. It does say that James spoke the decisive words and formulated the decision. In this situation he was at least as important and influential as Peter; indeed, the man who makes the crucial speech and formulates the actual decision really has the best claim to the credit for playing the leading role at the meeting.

The only serious challenge to this view of the decisive role of James at the conference is that he is said in Acts to have quoted Amos 9:11-12 in a form found not in the Hebrew but rather in the Septuagint. It is generally assumed, and no doubt rightly, that the Jerusalem conference was conducted in Aramaic, and we would expect James to quote the Hebrew form of the text. So it is questioned whether this speech comes from James at all. But the actual wording of this as of every other speech in Acts is the work of Luke, who in reporting the position taken by James writes in Greek and naturally uses the Greek translation of the Amos passage. It may be added that even the Hebrew text, though it sounds more nationalistic than the Greek version, nevertheless promises the inclusion of Gentile nations in the restored Davidic kingdom, and so fits the point of the speech as Luke gives it.

But the real point in the speech is that James approved the Gentile mission and spoke against requiring that Gentile believers be circumcised and keep the Mosaic Law. Paul in Galatians 2:6-10 explicitly says that James agreed to a Gentile mission in which Paul would not require Gentile believers to observe the Mosaic Law. This is essentially what the book of Acts reports that James said at the Jerusalem conference. Whether this conference in Acts 15 is to be identified with the one described in Galatians 2:1-10 is much disputed and must be discussed further when we take up the subject of "Paul and the Gentile Mission." Just now we are concerned with the position of James on the obligations of Gentiles who believe in Christ, and on that point Acts and Paul are in essential agreement. James recognized that the Gentile mission of Paul and Barnabas was legitimate; he defended the freedom of Gentile converts—they must not be required to keep the Mosaic Law.

There was a circumcision party in the Jerusalem church (Acts 11:2), and it stirred up trouble in the Antioch church (Acts 15:1). But neither Peter nor James belonged to that party. They agreed with Paul and Barnabas that Gentile believers did not have to keep the Mosaic Law, as Jews were accustomed to do. We may take this as solid historical fact.

In taking this position, however, James did not intend to release Jewish Christians from the obligation to observe the Mosaic Law. And by implication he did not think that he himself was released from that obligation. The special working of God among Gentiles in the now begun transition period at the end of this age he evidently recognized as quite proper and as not subject to the long standing system of Jewish observance, but he regarded Jews as under the Law until the final Kingdom should come.

It is possible that James traveled about visiting Jewish Christian groups. The one suggestion of this is in 1 Corinthians 9:5. There it is indicated that the brothers of the Lord were married, that they traveled about at the expense of the churches, and that the expense account in each case included the expenses of both the man and his wife. In no other passage does the New Testament suggest that James ever left Jerusalem after he came there at the start of the apostolic church (Acts 1:14), and it may be that in spite of Paul's inclusive statement it was only the other brothers of Jesus who thus traveled about to visit Jewish Christian groups in other cities. In any case, our major impression about James is that he remained in Jerusalem, at least as far as his regular practice was concerned, and that he was the leading figure there after Peter left the city at the time noted in Acts 12:17.

THE JEWISH LAW FOR JEWISH CHRISTIANS

But the influence of James extended beyond Jerusalem. Paul gives an unpleasant bit of evidence on that point. Paul and Barnabas were at Antioch in Syria. It is not said when this event occurred, but in the context it would seem to have been after the Jerusalem conference (Gal. 2:1-10). Peter came to Antioch, approved the spirit and the practice of the Christians there, and ate with the integrated church without attempting to keep all the ceremonial food rules of the Jewish Law. Then "certain men came from James" (Gal. 2:12). It is often argued that in fact they came on their own responsibility and had no instructions from James. That is not the impression given by Paul's words: He implies that they represented James and could speak for him.

It seems clear what the representatives of James had to say. They did not question the right of Gentiles to believe in Christ, and they did not demand that Gentiles should keep the Mosaic Law. What they wanted was for Jews who had believed in Christ to continue to keep that Law, and this the Jewish believers at Antioch were not doing.

For James and his messengers it was not enough that Jewish members of the church observe the four points mentioned in the agreement reached at the Jerusalem conference (Acts 15:29). Presumably those points were being observed by all of the Christians at Antioch. But in the view of James those points were for Gentiles to observe. The Jewish members of the church were to observe *all* requirements of the Mosaic Law. At Jerusalem James was living in a 100% Jewish Christian church, and he thought of the law-free Gentile churches as separate from the Jewish Christian congregations. He probably had not anticipated common table fellowship of Jewish and Gentile disciples, or if he had, he expected the Jewish ceremonial Law to control the practice in such a case.

Under pressure from the messengers sent by James, the Apostle Peter drew back and stopped eating with the Gentile Christians in the Antioch church. Then the other Jewish believers in the Antioch church, influenced by the messengers and especially by Peter's change of position, broke off their previous table fellowship with the Gentile believers. Finally even Barnabas, although he had been with Paul on the Gentile mission and, earlier, had led in the reception of Gentiles into the Antioch church, stopped eating with his Gentile brothers in faith. Of the Antioch Christians of Jewish ancestry Paul alone was left in active table fellowship with the Gentile Christians.

Our concern at this point is to learn what we can about the attitude of James and his reasons for it. He had a clear position. He approved preaching to Gentiles and did not think that they must keep the Mosaic Law. But it seems clear from Acts 15:21 that he expected synagogue worship to go on in every city and that he also expected Jewish Christians to keep the Mosaic Law. He expected all Jews who became Christians to continue to keep that Law.

This conclusion is confirmed by the one remaining passage in Acts in which James is mentioned. It refers to the time of Paul's final visit to Jerusalem (Acts 21:17-26). James is the outstanding leader of the Jerusalem church. He and the elders receive Paul in a formal way. James speaks to Paul of the numerous converts won from among the Jews in Jerusalem and elsewhere (the Greek phrase in verse 20 means "how many myriads or tens of thousands"). He tells Paul that these converts are zealous in keeping and defending the Mosaic Law. He reports to Paul that the Jewish Christians are saying that Paul is a renegade and teaches Jewish converts in the Dispersion not to keep the Mosaic Law. Then he appeals to Paul to prove that this report is false by joining four Jewish Christians then under a vow and paying the expenses they would have when formally concluding the period of this vow. This, James points out, would show that Paul himself keeps the Law.

Some have questioned whether Paul could have gone along with this proposal; it seems to clash with his gospel of grace and freedom from the Law. Indeed, from our later vantage point it does look strange. But it was possible for Paul. His normal way of life, when no threat to the unity of the church was involved, was Jewish. Moreover, among Jews he felt free to live in their way: "To the Jews I became as a Jew" (1 Cor. 9:20). And he always went as far as possible to avoid a split between Jerusalem and his Gentile churches.

This proposal of James to Paul shows us just what James wanted of all Jews who became Christians; they should keep the Law themselves, though they had no right to require Gentile converts to do so. And when we read Acts 15:13-21 carefully, we see that, in suggesting the agreement which the Jerusalem conference adopted, the real concern of James was not to require anything of Gentile Christians but to protect Jewish Christians from ceremonial laxity and defilement. Insofar as the Gentile Christians wanted to live in close fellowship with Jewish Christians, they should keep some simple regulations intended to avoid openly compromising their Jewish Christian fellow believers, but Jewish Christians were to keep the entire Mosaic Law and not just a few regulations. This was what James, who had no personal experience with churches containing both Jews and Gentiles, thought was necessary.

It is this consistent faithfulness to the ceremonial Law which I do not find at all in the Letter of James, and therefore I have not used that Letter in reconstructing the career of James the brother of Jesus. Some other arguments for assigning the Letter to a later date and another writer are not decisive. The good Greek of the Letter could be explained as due to an able secretary; that the brother of Jesus could write such good Greek is conceivable but not likely, and a helper in composing the Letter would be a better hypothesis. The relatively late date at which the Letter became known and accepted in the church is on the whole unfavorable to a date during the lifetime of the brother of the Lord, who was martyred in A.D. 62. The insistence in James 2:14-26 on the necessity of works for justification seems to me to reflect the Pauline controversies over justification by faith apart from works of the Law; for this reason I could not date the Letter about A.D. 45, as some do, and it seems to me less convincing to date it about A.D. 60, and take it as an attack on Paul's teaching by James the brother of Jesus, than it does to date it some decades later and understand it as the work of an unknown author who was not at all interested in the Jewish ceremonial Law, but rather wanted to answer a garbled Paulinism which was not clear as to the necessary ethical vitality of true faith. The Letter has no such concern for Jewish Christian observance of ceremonial Law as we find embodied in the career of James the brother of Jesus.

THE FADING ROLE OF JERUSALEM

Up to the time of Paul's final visit to Jerusalem, it must have seemed that Jerusalem was the center of the Christian church and was destined to remain so. There were ominous words of Jesus about the impending destruction of the Temple (cf. Mark 13:2 and parallels). Like the prophets of the Old Testament period, he had seen where the perverseness among his people was leading them. He had rejected Zealotism; his disciples who had been of Zealot inclinations had turned from them to follow him; he had seen what such a Zealot mood would bring upon his people. But we get no hint from Acts that the Jerusalem church thought of Jerusalem as doomed to early destruction. God's warnings of judgment had always been subject to alteration in the face of penitent response by his people.

So we need not think that the Jerusalem church lived under constant dread of impending disaster for themselves or for "the holy city." And for Jewish Christians the city and the Temple of Jerusalem had a special importance, and the Jerusalem church must have seemed the geographical center of the new Israel. In the church at large there was no rival for this honor.

But a relentless development had been going on almost unnoticed. There was an eschatological atmosphere in the message of Jesus, and the eschatological expectation was that Gentiles would find their place in God's final Kingdom. Jesus himself did almost nothing to bring Gentiles into his group, but he looked forward to this development. By word and example he seems to have given something of a pattern which Paul later used: ". . . to the Jew first and also to the Greek" (Rom. 1:16). The earliest church felt strongly the centrality of Israel and Jerusalem and recognized the right of the Jews to hear at once the full gospel, including the witness to the Resurrection and to the Lordship and Messiahship of Jesus. Yet the book of Acts is trustworthy in reflecting an implicit note of universalism even in the earliest days of the church; the eschatological climax had begun and so it was time for the work of God to broaden out to include all men. ". . . I will pour out my Spirit upon all flesh . . ."; ". . . whoever calls on the name of the Lord shall be saved"; ". . . the promise is to . . . every one whom the Lord our God calls to him" (Acts 2:17, 21, 39).

But it was not so much in the group of the Twelve as in the circle of the Seven, the Hellenistic Jews who became disciples, that the tie with the current institutions of Judaism was first openly and seriously questioned. Jesus and Peter had already questioned and challenged the existing official leadership of the Jews. But Stephen represented a challenge much deeper and far-reaching, for he—developing hints from Jesus—questioned the essential place of the Jerusalem Temple and its sacrifices. The death of Stephen and the scattering of those who shared his concerns gave to the surviving Jerusalem church a more conservative tone, and these developments constituted a mental pressure on the remaining members of the church to be careful about accepting any ideas that would clash with existing Judaism.

Peter and John, and by implication James the son of Zebedee, had caught from Jesus a certain breadth of outlook and of spirit, and while it was not so marked in them as in Stephen, it made them the target of the radical conservative Jews once Stephen and his group were removed from the scene. So James the son of Zebedee was martyred, Peter was imprisoned and was forced to leave Jerusalem, and it may be that the Apostle John left Jerusalem at the same time.

This left James the brother of Jesus as the leader. He was no Stephen. And he was no Peter. But he shared with them a breadth of outlook; while he expected the Jewish Christians to continue to keep the Mosaic Law, he was ready to accept Gentiles into the church without requiring them to be circumcised and keep that Law. James himself was loyal to the Law and to the Temple. He was respected by many Jews even outside his own group. Both Josephus, the first-century Jewish historian, in his *Antiquities,* XX.9.1, and Hegesippus, as quoted by Eusebius, attest these facts.[1]

But the opposition was closing in. In the Jerusalem church itself, as Acts 15:1, 5, shows, there were those who strongly disapproved of his position. They expected him not only to keep the Law, not only to require Jewish Christians to keep it, but also to require all Gentile converts to keep it. And this discontent with his view must have been even greater among the Jews outside the church who knew that he was ready to consider as Christians Gentiles who did not keep the Law. The outcome was his martyrdom, in A.D. 62, at the hands of fanatical Jews. We know of this martyrdom from Josephus and from Christian writers, and we have the report that prominent Jewish leaders, especially the Pharisees, protested this unlawful act to the incoming Roman governor, whose delayed arrival had given opportunity for the killing to be done without interference.

In the last analysis, however, there was a certain logic in the martyrdom of James. It took its place in a relentless sequence of events. Jesus had not been able to find a safe place within existing Judaism. Stephen could not. James the son of Zebedee could not, and neither could Peter except by withdrawing from Jerusalem and becoming a missionary to Jews in other places. Finally, the conservative James, the brother of Jesus, was found too troublesome to tolerate within the bounds of Judaism. His death marks the end of a process which said in effect that there was no place within Jewish circles for a Christian who would not insist that every Christian in the entire church must accept and observe the Jewish Law.

THE JERUSALEM CHURCH MOVES TO PELLA

There was one more step to take, and it was not long delayed. Four years after James the brother of Jesus had died, the

1. See Eusebius, *Church History,* II.23.

Jewish revolt against Rome broke out and led to the destruction of Jerusalem and its Temple. The Jewish Christians in Jerusalem left the city. Eusebius reports that they did so in obedience to an oracle, a divinely given instruction.[2] Was this a saying of Jesus somewhat like Mark 13:14, or was it, as Eusebius seems to imply, a prophetic utterance by some member of the Jerusalem church who felt prompted to instruct his fellow Christians to leave the doomed city at once? We cannot be certain, but the statement that they left and went across the Jordan to Pella, a short distance southeast of the Sea of Galilee, may be accepted as historical.

Eusebius gives no reason why they left Jerusalem except that the church was so instructed. But the step had its logic. It had become increasingly clear that the center of the Christian movement was in Jesus Christ, a center quite different from the centering of Judaism in the Law and the Temple. Just as it was the personal claim of Jesus which in the end was the real issue in the cleavage between him and the Jewish leaders, so at the end of the apostolic church's life in Jerusalem it was this same claim for Jesus, now made more explicitly in the light of his Resurrection and exaltation, that was the ground of the final break.

Christianity could not be true to itself and be merely a slightly supplemented and altered Judaism. Authentic Christianity fulfilled the Old Testament and gave a new center to life; it not only fulfilled but also replaced the Temple and its services; it not only fulfilled but also replaced the Law and the ancestral Jewish way of life. It brought far more than a supplement of this Jewish heritage; it brought a radical recasting of the center, focus, and pattern of Israel's life and mission.

Jewish Christianity, with its progressive narrowing of outlook and its increased emphasis on the distinctive Jewish observances, did not satisfy the Jews or express the real nature and scope of the gospel. The successive concessions of Jewish Christianity to Judaism did not further the cause of Christ; they only withdrew the Jewish Christians from the outgoing movement of the gospel and doomed Jewish Christianity to final

2. See his *Church History*, III.5.3.

defeat and disappearance. The conservative Jewish Christians were not able to present a gospel that really put the living Christ in the center of the message and let him shape the worship, fellowship, and community relationships of the church. Whether or not the Jewish Christians who fled from Jerusalem knew the implications of their action, their flight sounded the death knell of a Jewish Christianity whose main concern was to conform to the framework of surrounding Judaism. The series of steps by which the Jewish Christians tried to combine existing Judaism with the Christian confession had led to failure.

The Jewish Christian wing of the church finally could not avoid the break with Judaism. Both official Judaism and the church claimed the final authority, and both could not be right. The church had to break out of the pattern of Judaism to live. Gentile Christianity had done so earlier; the Jewish Christians, after a series of attempted adaptations to existing Judaism, failed to achieve the hoped-for working relation with that Judaism and had no healthy future.

THE ISOLATION AND DECLINE OF JEWISH CHRISTIANITY

The flight of the Jerusalem church to Pella was not only the symbol of the failure of the church to find a way to live peacefully within existing Judaism. It was also the event which cut the Gentile church loose from Jerusalem and the Jewish Christian church.

Up to this time the Jerusalem church had constituted the visible symbol of the unity of the church. No rival place had emerged to serve as such a symbol. The history of the Old Testament kingdom of David and the existence of the Jerusalem church had bound Gentile Christians to their Jewish Christian friends in a common geographical tie. But when the Jewish Christians left Jerusalem, and even more when Jerusalem was actually destroyed by the Romans, that uniting symbol was gone. Lost was the geographical bond that preserved to some extent the sense of unity between the Jewish and the Gentile Christians. A group in Pella could not capture the imagination of Gentile Christians in the way that the church in Jerusalem had done.

When Paul took the great collection to Jerusalem at the close of his missionary activity (Rom. 15:25-28), he had as one major purpose to keep Jewish and Gentile Christians bound in mutual love and visible unity. Such measures could no longer succeed. The Jewish Christian church was isolated from its Gentile Christian brothers. The Gentile Christian churches no longer felt a close tie with Jerusalem or with Jewish Christians.

This was a real loss for the Gentile Christian churches. But it was a greater loss for the Jewish Christian group. They had cast in their lot with the Jewish communities, and had accommodated their way of life to them as far as they could without complete surrender of their faith in Jesus as Messiah. The result was to separate them from the Gentile Christian churches without giving them any real home within Judaism. Their flight from Jerusalem must have increased Jewish nationalist hostility to them. They were spiritual orphans with no real future.

That is how we see the result today. The Jewish Christians could not foresee what was to come. They continued their Jewish way of life and their confession of faith in Jesus as the Christ. They continued their witness within Judaism in the conditions that followed the fall of Jerusalem. We do not know much about their history. But scattered references to them in the rabbinical tradition are sufficient to show that they continued their life in Palestine, including Galilee; they engaged in discussions with rabbis, and continued an evangelistic program among Jews. In the second century, though some of them lived west of the Jordan River, their center of strength apparently was still in Transjordan. They were widely called "Ebionites," a name which seems to mean that they were known as "the poor" (cf. Gal. 2:10). They did not follow the Gentile church's development of a New Testament canon, but were content with the Old Testament and one Gospel. In general they did not develop as high a Christology as did the Gentile churches, and as a group they seem to have rejected the virgin birth. There was a strong tendency in Jewish Christianity to develop a bitter polemic against Paul, who was regarded as the great apostate and betrayer of the Law.

As time went on they developed various trends. Some scholars think that they received influences from members of the Qumran sect who fled from Qumran about A.D. 68. Some Jewish Christians evidently adapted more or less to syncretistic ways of thought and practice; the evidence of Jewish features in Gnostic developments of the second and third centuries need not come in all cases directly from Judaism, but may often have roots in centrifugal tendencies in Jewish Christianity. But our information about later Jewish Christianity is meager, confused, and difficult to weave into a connected story.

The Jewish Christian movement lasted on at least into the fourth century, but it had no effective tie with Gentile churches and no great influence on Judaism. Because it had not been willing to recast all of its thought and practice in the light of the work and Lordship of Jesus Christ, because it had let the legal requirements of current Judaism dominate its life and relationships, it had no vital growing power; and though it held on for many generations, it dwindled away and disappeared. It had the sort of fate which can happen to any section of the church which lets its life be shaped and controlled by national and cultural ties instead of finding in Jesus Christ the judgment on all existing ties and the Redeemer and Transformer of all inherited ways of life.

V

Paul and the Gentile Mission

For the author of the book of Acts the Apostle Paul was the outstanding figure in the history of the apostolic church. He is mentioned in twenty-one of the twenty-eight chapters, and in the last sixteen chapters is continuously on stage. Except for a brief scene in which Paul and James meet (21:18-25), Paul is the only prominent Christian leader to appear in the last thirteen chapters. The conclusion is inevitable that, for the writer of Acts, Paul is the dominant figure of the story.

It is true that we are not dependent on Acts alone for our understanding of the ministry and the significance of Paul. This is fortunate, since the account in Acts is fragmentary. For example, it never once hints that Paul was a brilliant, resourceful letter writer who by his Letters contributed to the spiritual guidance of his newly founded churches. Acts gives but a meager reflection of the devoted and effective pastoral ministry which Paul fulfilled in his churches; the book is concerned with the expansion and apologetic defense of the gospel rather than with the growth and problems of the individual mission churches. Fortunately for us, these internal problems of Paul's churches are precisely the matters with which almost all of his Letters deal. Acts also gives us but limited insight into the magniture of the theological contribution which Paul made to his own day and was to make to the later church. We therefore are grateful that so many of his Letters have been preserved. They contribute immensely to our knowledge of how Paul worked and how he understood and interpreted the gospel.

THE PORTRAIT OF PAUL IN ACTS

This does not mean that Acts tells us but little about Paul. Let us see how it presents him and his role in the apostolic church:

1. The book of Acts presents Paul as a passionately dedicated man. At every stage of his career he is completely devoted to the faith he professes. He is never neutral; he is always active in his religious loyalty (cf., e.g., Acts 26:1-29). For this reason he seems strange to many modern Christians. We have been taught that the ideal is to be a well-balanced, normal, and satisfactorily adjusted personality. We do not know what to do with a man who is a fanatic, a rabid, restless, unceasing partisan of the message which he is convinced should be the one urgent concern for every right-minded person. Luke pictures Paul as a man who gives himself completely to the defense and the advance of the faith he professes. No one who thinks of faith as merely a mildly stimulating and moderately influential factor in life will ever understand Paul.

2. The book of Acts presents Paul as a trained man, educated for religious leadership. He had been ". . . brought up in this city [Jerusalem] at the feet of Gamaliel, educated according to the strict manner of the law of our fathers" (Acts 22:3). He put his intellect and training at the service of Christ and the Christian mission.

We often hear praise of the Apostles as a group of "uneducated, common men" (Acts 4:13). It is true that the Twelve were not rabbis; they had nothing like a B.D. degree. And they rendered a real and noble service without such formal training for Christian leadership. But the extent of their contribution is often overstated. As we have seen in our study of Acts, Peter is the only one of the Twelve who makes a vigorous individual contribution. Of the six outstanding leaders of the apostolic church (Peter, Barnabas, Stephen, Philip, James the brother of Jesus, and Paul), Peter is the only one from the Twelve. On the other hand, we must not pretend that the other five outstanding leaders all had rabbinical training; that is highly improbable. But the one great theologian and pioneer of the world church, Paul, did have such training, and this fact deserves attention.

3. The book of Acts presents Paul as a loyal Jew. For that matter, so do the Letters of Paul. It was his conviction and the conviction of the early church that Jesus had fulfilled the promises to Israel and that the gift of the Spirit to the church and to the Spirit-guided life of the church was likewise the fulfillment of Old Testament promises. The church was the true Israel, and while the new decisive acts of God brought a real advance in God's working, so that the church could think of itself as the *new* Israel, it was still God's people Israel. Paul was deeply devoted to his people, preached to them whenever occasion offered, and prayed for their salvation through Christ. He never thought of himself as outside the bounds of Israel. It never occurred to him that he was not a Jew; he was a true Jew, proud of his heritage and sure that God's gracious power and plan would yet bring his people into the church and the final Kingdom (cf. Acts 22:3: "I am a Jew . . ." and also 26:6). If there were Jews disloyal to their heritage and their God, it was those who rejected Jesus Christ and persecuted the church. Paul himself never lost his sense of being a loyal member of God's people Israel.

4. The book of Acts presents Paul as a persecutor of the church. People do not bother to persecute persons or movements of no significance. Paul sensed in the Christian group a threat to the Jewish life as he was living it in his pre-Christian days. In part this threat may have seemed to him to be due to a laxity which Christians were showing toward the Mosaic Law and the Jewish ceremonies. But his main concern was probably the high claim that the disciples were making for Jesus. We cannot recover the full facts concerning Paul's persecuting activity and his reason for it. But I think it plausible to hold that part of the

background of Paul's later Christology rooted in this persecuting period. Paul knew that the Christians put before him a fundamental choice. They made a radical criticism of his Pharisaic way of life; they made a claim for Jesus which if accepted would radically change his own faith and life (cf. Acts 9:20). At that stage he thought that the disciples were misguided, and that their misguided preaching was dangerous to the health and the future of Judaism, and so he acted with great earnestness to stamp out the threatening movement (Acts 9:1-2; 22:4-5; 26:9-11).

5. The book of Acts presents Paul as a convert. Such a statement can be misunderstood. In a real sense, Paul did not think that he had given up his Jewish faith and his place in the life of Israel. He was still a Jew; he still accepted the Jewish Scriptures; he thought of his new faith as the faith which all Israel should share; the disciples therefore constituted the true Israel. But the change of center, the acceptance of Jesus as the Christ, the Son of God (cf. Acts 9:20), the giving of his life to Christ in complete dedication, was so radical a change that nothing less than the word "conversion" will do it justice. For all of his grateful recognition of the continuity of the new faith with the Old Testament and the life of Israel, he was keenly aware of the newness of the Christian message that he now accepted.

Most of us have grown up in the church. We have been taught from childhood to accept the gospel and the Bible witness to it, and the Christian position seems to us natural and inevitable. The convert who has to make a radical break with his past way of life in order to become a Christian and join the Christian fellowship is likely to be more clearly aware of how new, important, and urgent the gospel is. The recognition of that newness and urgency may come to any of us as we really grasp how great a judgment the gospel pronounces on other ways of life and how rich a gift God gives to faith. But the convert who has to make a complete change of life can never escape this sense of how new and how crucially important his faith is. For Paul the miracle of the privilege of faith in Christ was always a cause of wonder to him. He could never take it for granted; he could only rejoice and be grateful for it.

6. The book of Acts presents Paul as an evangelistic preacher. His consuming concern was to win as many as possible to a genuine faith in Jesus Christ (cf. Acts 26:29). His Letters show that he knew clearly how greatly new converts, especially those who came into the church from pagan life, needed growth and guidance, and we have noted that his Letters show a pastoral concern for all his churches. But he was conscious that his own distinctive mission was to preach the gospel to those whose lives had not yet been gripped by it; his primary task was to win converts (Acts 26:16-20).

We often hear condescending remarks about ministers who are concerned for mere numbers. Numbers were never "mere" for Paul. He was out to win as many men as possible to faith in Christ. His method was not that of the discussion panel or that of the slow diffusion of Christian influence. Time was limited and the number of people to be reached was great. He felt driven to get quickly to the point and appeal for decision, and he could never forget how many people still needed to be reached by his message. His characteristic work was that of an itinerant evangelist.

7. The book of Acts presents Paul as a missionary who did not ignore the Jews but went mainly to the Gentiles. In doing this he developed a geographical strategy which would enable him to reach as many Gentiles as possible. I remember once reading a book on Paul which described his turning from the Jews to the Gentiles at Pisidian Antioch (Acts 13:46-47); this was presented as a radical change in Paul's method. Yet in Iconium, the very next city which Paul visited, he went first to the synagogue (Acts 14:1), and this was his regular pattern to the very end of the story, for even in Rome his first concern was to speak to the rulers of the synagogue in that city (Acts 28:17-28). To him the church was one, and the Jews should hear the gospel. But his own special work was to preach the gospel to the Gentiles. As a missionary he felt a particular responsibility to them.

Moreover, Paul was a missionary in that he deliberately tried to avoid working where others had already founded churches. His work, he felt, was to preach where others had not preached;

the narrative of Acts documents this policy, which Romans 15:20 shows us was deliberately followed. As a missionary he developed the strategy of centering his work in the main cities and letting his influence spread out into the surrounding regions. Visitors to the city who heard him could take the gospel to neighboring areas (Acts 19:10), and his assistants could move out to lesser cities in the region. He definitely aimed to reach the greatest number possible in a relatively short time. He took care to revisit his churches when possible, but as a missionary his main interest after founding a church in a city was to move on to another pioneer work.

8. The book of Acts presents Paul as an apologist, that is, as an intelligent Christian active to defend and explain his faith and make it persuasive, especially to those in positions of authority.

As we have noted, it is at first sight amazing that the story of the expansion of the church breaks off at Acts 19:20, and the last nine and a half chapters deal with Paul's last journey to Jerusalem and his voyage to Rome. Thus this last journey of Paul occupies more space in Acts than does all that Acts tells of apostolic mission work outside of Palestine.

To Luke this last journey of Paul and the speeches in it were of great importance for his purpose. That purpose included much more than the exaltation of Paul or the satisfaction of biographical interest. It recognized that Paul was more than an isolated individual. He represented the cause which his ministry had been serving. His progress was symbolic of the general progress of the gospel. His imprisonment was a threat to the church and a symbol of the challenge which both Jews and Gentiles were making to the gospel. His defense was a defense of the gospel, and the recognitions by the Roman military and civil leaders that he was innocent of crime against the state were to Luke valid apologies for the church.

These last nine and a half chapters are thus largely in the nature of an apology, and they show that for Luke the defense of Paul was linked with the defense of the gospel. Paul's speeches in these chapters show that his life record was not marred by crime or rebellion, that his religious roots were in Judaism, which Rome recognized as a legitimate faith, and that his Christian faith was the fulfillment of God's promises to Israel and so was as legitimate before the law as Rome had recognized Judaism to be. No valid charge against him had ever been made, and his innocence of crime had been recognized repeatedly by Roman officials. Thus Luke presents Paul as an effective apologist, a spokesman for his faith who was never convincingly answered.

9. The book of Acts presents Paul as the apostolic sponsor of the church at Rome. There were Christians in Rome when Paul arrived there; in fact, Luke tells us that they met him as he came on the road from Puteoli to Rome (Acts 28:15). Paul's Letter to the Romans makes it clear that a strong and widely known church had existed there for years before he reached the city. Who founded the Roman church we do not know. Its origin may go back to a time only a few weeks or months after Pentecost, when converted "visitors from Rome" returned home (Acts 2:10).

One negative statement which all good evidence supports is that Peter did not found the Roman church. Indeed, the narrative of Acts indicates that Luke knew of no activity of Peter in Rome prior to the arrival of Paul. For Luke the apostolic preaching which gave the Roman church a solid sponsor was that of Paul the prisoner. Whether Peter went to Rome later, as tradition says and as I think probable, Luke does not tell us. But the implication of the close of Acts is that Peter had not been in Rome and was not in Rome when Paul reached that city. It was Paul's preaching which for Luke effectively established and directly attested the apostolic preaching in Rome.

10. The book of Acts may hint that Paul died a martyr death for Christ. To the elders of Ephesus Paul says that they will see his face no more (Acts 20:25, 38). This could mean that his martyr death lay close ahead; it could be Luke's way of hinting at Paul's death without making it the climax of Acts. To have described Paul's execution might have made it seem to parallel or to rival in importance the crucifixion of Jesus.

Certainly Paul did suffer for his faith. Acts tells of various hardships and persecutions which he underwent, although it does not tell the whole story, whose full range is suggested by the astounding series of varied hardships which Paul recalls in 2 Corinthians 11:24-27. But the book of Acts is not a clear witness of Paul's martyr death. We first hear explicitly of that martyrdom in ancient church tradition.

* * *

These are ways in which Acts shows us the many-sided personality, ministry, and experience of Paul. They may help us to see his place in the development of the Gentile mission. It is only in keeping with his own intent to view his work as a part of the total movement to take the gospel to the world. This total mission, as Acts 1:8 makes clear, is really the theme of the book of Acts, and it is obviously essential to the purpose of Acts to show that Paul had the most prominent and effective role in realizing that world outreach of the gospel. It is appropriate, therefore, to conclude our study of Acts with a careful study of the rise and development of the Gentile mission and Paul's place in that history.

JESUS AND THE GENTILE MISSION

One assumption often made must be challenged at the outset of a study of the rise of the Gentile mission. This is the assumption that the church in Jerusalem started out as a Jewish Christian group of strict legalistic practice, and that only after hard struggle did a freer attitude emerge to shape the course of events. I am convinced that this viewpoint is radically wrong. The situation at the beginning of the Apostolic Age was not rigid. It was not fully clarified. The thread of universalism was present from the first. And it had its roots in the attitude and the teaching of Jesus.

To get the proper background for the first years of the Apostolic Age it is only right to include a study of the Gospels.

Jesus confined his ministry almost entirely to the Jews. It is not only the Gospel of Matthew which shows this. This Gospel does indeed emphasize this picture of a limited ministry: Jesus says, "I was sent only to the lost sheep of the house of Israel" (Matt. 15:24), and he tells his disciples to "Go nowhere among the Gentiles, and enter no town of the Samaritans, but go rather to the lost sheep of the house of Israel" (Matt. 10:5-6). But the same limitation of his ministry almost exclusively to the Jews is found in Mark and Luke and John.

In all four Gospels, however, the constant concern of Jesus is for a type of faith and obedience to God which gives a minimum of place to the legalistic, ceremonial, and divisive aspects of Jewish life. Even the Gospel of Matthew, whose strongly Jewish background is so often stressed by scholars, gives glimpses of a wider horizon. The coming of the wise men prefaces the gospel story with a note of the world relevance of the coming of Jesus (Matt. 2:1), and the closing command to "Go therefore and make disciples of all nations . . ." (Matt. 28:19) opens up a view of the full Gentile mission. In the teaching of Jesus this Gospel quotes Jesus as saying that ". . . many will come from east and west and sit at table with Abraham, Isaac, and Jacob in the kingdom of heaven . . ." (Matt. 8:11), a saying which has an essential parallel in Luke 13:28-29. Thus the Gospel of Matthew, like the other Gospels, shows frankly that, while Jesus limited his ministry almost entirely to the Jews, he expected his gospel to be carried to the Gentiles and anticipated that all nations would share in the coming Kingdom.

But while it has been important to note this viewpoint in the Gospel of Matthew, it is of immediate relevance for our purpose to study its place in the Gospel of Luke. To learn how Luke understood the earliest attitude of the apostolic church it is not only legitimate but necessary to ask what position his Gospel presents. This Gospel emphasizes the loyalty of Jesus to his people. It gives prominence to Jerusalem and the Temple at the beginning (Luke 1:8-9), and specifies at the end that Jerusalem is to be the starting point of the church's world mission (Luke

24:47, 53). But it introduces from the start hints that the outreach of the gospel message is to be universal.

Simeon speaks of Jesus as "a light for revelation to the Gentiles" as well as "for glory to thy people Israel" (Luke 2:32). In quoting Isaiah concerning John the Baptist's ministry, Luke is the only evangelist who extends the quotation to include the promise that "all flesh shall see the salvation of God" (Luke 3:4-6, quoting Isa. 40:3-5). Luke, like Matthew, has the saying of Jesus that the Law is not discarded, but, again like Matthew, has the saying that since the time of John the Baptist a new order has come, and it is obvious that this is understood as a nonlegalistic order (Luke 16:16-17; cf. Matt. 5:17-18; 11:12-13).

There is in the Gospel of Luke no racial exclusivism, no ceremonial emphasis, no legalistic note, and no divisive spirit (a Samaritan can be the hero, humanly speaking, in a parable in which Jewish leaders come off badly; Luke 10:25-37). While Luke in the eschatological discourse does not parallel the specific statement that the gospel must first be preached to all nations (cf. Matt. 24:14; Mark 13:10), the conclusion of his Gospel gives the instruction of the risen Christ that ". . . repentance and forgiveness of sins should be preached in his name to all nations, beginning from Jerusalem" (Luke 24:47).

It may be said that these hints of a coming universalistic mission program are additions to the original gospel tradition and were created only after the Gentile mission had developed. In reply, it should be said that all four Gospels agree in this outlook, that Jesus by all accounts downgraded the divisive, legalistic, and ceremonial aspects, that he treated such aspects as dispensable in his relations with tax collectors and sinners, that he presented a gospel which without explicitly discarding the current Jewish legal framework of life did not require it, and that developments in the Apostolic Age can be understood much easier if the broader view rooted in sayings and attitudes of Jesus himself.

One more observation is important. Jesus worked with the keen awareness that in him and his movement the fulfillment of God's eschatological promises had begun. In that final working of God the Gentiles were widely expected to be included in a more direct way than had been the case before. To take seriously the eschatological significance of Jesus' ministry, death, Resurrection, and exaltation was to look for worldwide effects from that work; it inevitably directed attention to the Gentiles.

A partially realized eschatology, which is what I understand Jesus and the early church to represent, opened the way to inclusion of Gentiles in the new order. God had acted, and his action concerned all men. It might not be clear as yet just how this would affect the Gentiles. But the church did not begin with the conviction that the gospel was for Jews alone and that Gentiles had no place in it. Its initial atmosphere was not legalistic, ceremonial, and exclusive. According to all of our Gospels, and quite specifically according to the Gospel of Luke, the way was open for an outreaching development whose exact stages were not yet known.

THE WORLD OUTLOOK OF THE EARLIEST JERUSALEM CHURCH

The Pentecost story confirms this impression of a broad horizon (Acts 2:1-41). We may ask questions about that story, especially since the Gospel of John dates the gift of the Spirit on the evening of the Resurrection day (John 20:22). But the gift of the Spirit is one of the surest facts of the early church's experience. It had a universal implication. The Old Testament promise in Joel 2:28-32 is for a pouring out of God's Spirit "on all flesh," so that "all who call upon the name of the Lord shall be delivered" (cf. Acts 2:17-21). For Luke the gift of tongues symbolizes and confirms this universalistic range of the gift of the Spirit. This makes it likely that in Acts 2:39 Luke means to include Gentiles in "all that are far off, every one whom the Lord our God calls to him." As Acts 1:8 makes explicit, Luke understands the gift of the Spirit to involve a world mission.

Such a world mission was the only way to be true to the exalted role of the risen Christ. American Protestants have been widely accustomed to celebrating Easter and then relaxing until fall or winter before resuming interest in the church year. That, however, is an antibiblical procedure. No Christian celebrates Easter with proper understanding unless he also celebrates the ascension or exaltation of Jesus Christ and his gift of the Spirit at Pentecost. The celebration of Ascension Day recognizes that as the risen Christ he is the Lord. This title was no late invention of some Gentile Christian. It was the immediate and basic confession of the church; Jesus is "Lord and Christ" (Acts 2:36). This Lordship is not a merely local or Jewish rule; it has worldwide reference, and as we have said, so does the gift of the Spirit.

Thus the Gentile mission is implicit, to say the least, in the ascension or exaltation and in Pentecost. It is not surprising, therefore, to find Acts 3:26 saying that the gospel is being preached "to you [Jews] first," and to hear Peter say that ". . . there is salvation in no one else, for there is no other name under heaven given among men by which we must be saved" (Acts 4:12).

The conclusion to which all of these facts lead is that in the first period of the apostolic church, the earliest years at Jerusalem as described in Acts 1-5, the group of disciples, although living within the bounds of Judaism, lived in a nonlegalistic spirit and with a hope that had wide horizons. They saw that their immediate task was to give an effective witness to their fellow Jews. They had not really faced the question as to how the wider witness was to be given or how it was to begin.

THE FREE SPIRIT OF STEPHEN

In the book of Acts it is Stephen, or to put it more broadly, it is the Hellenistic Jews in the Jerusalem church, who most actively reflect the free spirit of Jesus and bring upon themselves the hostility of conservative Judaism. It is noteworthy that both the spearhead of the church and the basic opposition take form among Greek-speaking Jews (Acts 6:9).

The charge against Stephen is that he had spoken against the Temple and predicted its destruction, and that he had spoken against the Law. In both respects he is said to have echoed words of Jesus (Acts 6:13-14).

His so-called defense is not a personal defense but rather a withering criticism of a Judaism bound to one land, one city, a central Temple, and a system of animal sacrifices (Acts 7:1-53). The implication seems to be that the coming and work of Jesus has given to faith a new center and so has antiquated certain existing forms of worship, which in any case never had the sanction and importance commonly given to them. But Stephen is not said to have disowned the Law; he simply denounced the Jews for not keeping it, and while he was highly critical of the Temple, he apparently would have been satisfied to keep the "tent of witness" of which the Law spoke. He did not break loose from Judaism, but he did give a burning criticism of current views of holy land and holy place and holy sacrifices. Acceptance of his views would have meant a radical recasting of Jewish life to make Jesus, rather than these traditionally holy things, the center of Jewish faith, worship, and thought.

STEPS TO A WORLD MISSION

We must sense the free spirit in Stephen and his group, but we must stop short of saying that they saw clearly the rightness and necessity of the active mission to the Gentiles. There is no evidence that Stephen or his friends clearly saw this universal outreach, as Paul later did. In fact, one of the most striking things in Acts is its picture of a church slow to see this full range of the gospel message. It was a reluctant church, which only slowly moved into the full Gentile mission. Note the four stages or steps by which the church, originally composed solely of Jewish believers in Christ, was led by the unexpected course of events to take up that mission.

The first step was the preaching to the Samaritans (Acts 8:4-13). It was Philip, a member of the Seven, who took this step. He was driven from Jerusalem by persecution and led to go to Samaria, and the free spirit which he shared with Stephen led him to preach there. This step did not raise all the questions which the full Gentile mission had to face. The Samaritans, a racially mixed people, had Israelite blood in them, and they, like the Jews, recognized the Law as authoritative. To preach to them was a step which a church with a free spirit could take without facing all that might follow.

It is significant that when Philip took this step, the Jerusalem leaders did not condemn it, even though Stephen had been martyred and the Jerusalem church, or at least its Hellenistic wing, had been persecuted. They either accepted it or at least were ready to send Peter and John to consider the evidence and accept it if it seemed the working of God. Peter and John did accept it (Acts 8:14-25), although the idea that only the Twelve could confer the Spirit has no basis elsewhere in Acts. No traces of narrow legalism crop out in the story at this point, nor does it appear in the story of the conversion and baptism of the God-fearing Ethiopian eunuch (Acts 8:26-40).

The next step occurred when Peter preached to the Gentile household of Cornelius and baptized them without requiring them to accept the Jewish Law (Acts 10). As "a devout man who feared God" (Acts 10:2) Cornelius undoubtedly observed a few of the practices of Judaism, but he was not a Jew, did not accept the obligation to keep the entire Law, and his baptism was a new step in the movement of the church toward a full Gentile mission.

There is strong evidence that Peter was inwardly troubled by this turn of events, and a hint that he knew he was liable to be criticized by some of his fellow Christians. Should he be staying with a tanner, whose occupation was considered defiling (Acts 9:43)? Should he visit and eat in a Gentile home, even in one whose head was "a devout man who feared God"? His scruples were overcome; he went to the home of Cornelius. There the Holy Spirit pushed him further. The Spirit was given to the group of Gentiles. This for Peter was divine testimony that the Gentiles were acceptable just as the Jews were, without being required to be circumcised or keep the Jewish Law. It was not the sort of event in which Peter wanted to share every day, but he accepted it and defended it at Jerusalem (Acts 11:1-18).

Incidentally, the fact that he took Jewish believers with him from Joppa to Caesarea, and then took all six of them to Jerusalem to attest the genuineness of the Spirit's working in the lives of the Gentile household, shows that there was in the Jerusalem church a more conservative tendency, to which Peter did not belong but which he knew must be answered.

The third step was taken at Antioch in Syria (Acts 11:19-26). Disciples of Stephen's group came there and preached to Jews. Some of them, however, preached to pagan Gentiles, and found that such Gentiles also would believe the gospel. This was the first preaching to Gentiles who, as far as we can tell, had no previous connection with the synagogue. Again, as in Samaria, the church at Jerusalem felt a responsibility to investigate. But this time they did not send two Apostles; they did not send one of the Twelve at all; they sent instead a one-man committee, Barnabas. He was convinced that what had occurred was the work of God's Spirit (Acts 11:19-24). There is no hint that he acted to mediate the Spirit to the new church; it seems assumed that they had received the Spirit already.

There at Antioch was the natural place for the name "Christian" to arise as a designation of a disciple (Acts 11:26). It was the first time that Jews and Gentiles had united in one church without making thorough Jewish legal observance the basis of their community life. We know that there were Jews in this Antioch church (Gal. 2:11-14), and so it is clear that the Gentiles in it did not make up a solely Gentile church.

The fourth step was taken when a completely Gentile church was formed. It is not clear that this ever happened in the Apostolic Age. Whenever we have clear evidence about any local church in the Apostolic Age, it included Jews. On the missionary journeys of Paul and Barnabas, and later when Paul went alone on a further mission, it was common for the mission to be begun in a synagogue and later forced out of the synagogue into a direct appeal to pagan Gentiles. But on such occasions the missionaries undoubtedly took with them the Jews and synagogue-related Gentiles who had been won during the ministry in the synagogue. So it is very doubtful whether there ever was a purely Gentile church in the Apostolic Age. The church had reached the time when such a church was possible, but we cannot be sure that one actually was founded. Certainly Paul, with his deep loyalty to his fellow Jews, would have worked to include Jewish believers as the nucleus of any church he founded.

THE EMERGENCE OF THE CRISIS

The picture we have been painting is that of a church which had a certain freedom of spirit within an inherited Jewish pattern of religious worship and life. It was able to move toward a Gentile mission by successive stages. At first it did not have to face the ultimate questions involved, but as the trend became clearer, objections inevitably were voiced and increased in vigor. In such a development a time had to come when the whole trend was openly challenged by conservative Jewish believers who asserted the necessity of keeping the inherited Jewish way of life.

There is no evidence that the hostility to Stephen and his group came from within the church. When Peter preached in the house of Cornelius and baptized the Gentiles there without requiring them to adhere to the Jewish Law and practices, objection arose within the church, but it was effectively answered by the evidence that the Spirit had guided Peter in what he did (Acts 11:1-18). There was a question about the propriety of such preaching to pagan Gentiles as had occurred at Antioch in Syria, but this caused no major crisis; one man, not a member of the Twelve, was sent to investigate and to determine whether the development was acceptable, and while Barnabas no doubt reported favorably on this issue during the famine visit to Jerusalem by Barnabas and Saul (Acts 11:30), Luke gives no hint of a critical controversy at that time.

The picture in Acts—and it accords with what might be expected in such a development—is that the protest of conservative Jewish Christians became insistent and militant only when the increasing number of Gentiles in the church pointed to the time when Gentiles would constitute the majority. This crisis came when Barnabas and Saul had made a journey which not only showed Paul's capacity for leadership but also resulted in the conversion of considerable numbers of pagan Gentiles (Acts 13-14).

THE JERUSALEM CONFERENCE ON REQUIREMENTS FOR GENTILES

This crisis was settled in a way that kept the way open for an active mission to Gentiles. They were not required to become Jews and keep the Jewish laws and ceremonies. This solid fact is clear from all of the evidence.

There are, to be sure, many problems concerning the conference of Christian leaders at Jerusalem which faced this crisis. Paul's account of the meeting, in Galatians 2:1-10, was written in such agitation and in such broken sentences that it is not always possible to be sure of his meaning. In Acts it is not certain which of Paul's visits to Jerusalem is the one of which Galatians 2:1-10 speaks. Is it the famine visit in Acts 11:30? Or is it the visit in Acts 15:1-29, which actually tells of a conference? Or are these two apparently separate visits really variant accounts of the same visit? It still seems to me much more likely that Acts 15:1-29 tells of the same visit as Galatians 2:1-10. The basic issue was whether Gentiles who believed in Christ must be circumcised in order to be members of Christ's church. And on any reading of the evidence the essential result stands out clearly: Paul won his case; it was not required that Gentile Christians be circumcised and thereby accept in principle the obligation to keep the Mosaic Law.

Christians today usually fail to recognize the strength of the case presented by Paul's opponents. The opponents are not named. They did not include any known leaders of the Jerusalem church; in both Acts and Galatians not only Peter but even James the brother of Jesus came out on Paul's side. But whoever the opponents were, they were not arbitrary or capricious men. They could quote the literal text of Scripture for their side.

It seems to me certain that these opponents quoted, at least as part of their case, Genesis 17:9-14. This passage insists that circumcision is required of every descendant of Abraham and of every foreigner bought by a descendant of Abraham. This is called "an everlasting convenant." The passage concludes: "Any uncircumcised male who is not circumcised in the flesh of his foreskin shall be cut off from his people; he has broken my covenant." On a literal reading of Scripture, this is an airtight case for demanding circumcision of every Gentile who wants a place in the covenant people under Israel's Messiah.

If, as I would affirm, Paul saw more deeply when he argued that the faith of Abraham was the clue to what makes man acceptable to God, it still must be said that a real issue was honestly raised by Paul's opponents. How Paul answered these honest men I would like to know. They needed more of an answer than his argument that the promise to faith (Gen. 15:6) was earlier and so more basic than the covenant of circumcision (Gen. 17:9-14). Did he, as Peter had done in defending his baptism of Cornelius and his household, appeal also to the obviously Spirit-guided life and service of Titus, the Gentile he had taken with him to Jerusalem, quite possibly to use as "Exhibit A" of what God had done for and through Gentiles (Gal. 2:3)?

In any case, the three "pillars" (Gal. 2:9), James the brother of Jesus, Cephas or Peter, and John the son of Zebedee, agreed with Paul. The Gentiles need not be circumcised to be true Christians. Paul's Gentile mission was approved and could continue. Paul's teaching of salvation by grace through faith, apart from the keeping of the Law, was vindicated. Rarely in church history has a man won a more sweeping victory than Paul won on this occasion. Never was a victory won which was more essential to the health and future of the church.

THE AUTHORITY OF THE JERUSALEM CHURCH

This agreement at the Jerusalem conference is clear. But it leaves two questions to consider. One concerns the authority of the Jerusalem church. Luke describes the conference as a meeting in which the Apostles at Jerusalem, with the elders of that church, made the decision. We get the impression from Paul that he did not feel a bit inferior to the Jerusalem leaders. It is clear that he did recognize the *de facto* primacy of the Jerusalem church; he had to have that church's support or his mission work would at best be crippled (Gal. 2:2). But I think that he regarded himself as more of an equal with the Jerusalem leaders than the account of Acts may suggest to us. He would have insisted that he was not a subordinate appointee of the Jerusalem church, and he would have been right. But the Jerusalem church did have a kind of central authority, which to Luke and to most Christians would have justified the kind of picture which Acts paints.

It must be noted, however, that the authority of the Jerusalem church was not the authority of the Twelve in the simple way so often depicted. James the brother of Jesus was not one of the Twelve, yet he seems to have been the dominant Jerusalem figure at the conference, and Paul implies this by the order in which he lists the leaders in Galatians 2:9. The elders join in the negotiations and the decision and the letter with an air of authority. James the brother of Jesus, the Twelve as far as present, and the Jerusalem elders shared the leadership. And the Jerusalem church taken as a whole had at that time a practical primacy which Luke reflects. It was at Jerusalem that this problem had to be settled if the church was to continue as one effective church.

THE SO-CALLED "APOSTOLIC DECREE"

The other question relates to the so-called "decree," which says that Gentile Christians are to "abstain from what has been sacrificed to idols and from blood and from what is strangled and from unchastity" (Acts 15:29). A book could be written about this "decree." We must confine ourselves to a few observations. But I hope to put the matter in a light which I have not found in the many discussions of the question which I have read.

I would suggest first that the title "decree" is too legalistic a word to describe the agreement reached. The agreement reached and the message sent were not the product of such a formal situation as is implied by the word "decree." I would state next that I see no help in the idea, which once seemed preferable to me, that the "decree" was actually a regulation passed at Jerusalem at a time when Paul was not present, and that he first heard of it at the time of his last visit to Jerusalem (Acts 21:25). On that occasion, some contend, James tells Paul of the agreement, previously unknown to Paul. This certainly is not Luke's intention. In writing Acts 21:25 he is clearly referring back to Acts 15:29; he is not telling of something which Paul is now hearing for the first time.

If we accept Acts as giving in essentials a historical account, we have to date the agreement at the time of the conference in chapter 15, and ask what it meant in that situation. Did it mean a radical alteration in Paul's position? Did he, as is often implied, compromise his gospel of grace in an inconsistent and shameful way? Was it such a radical change of position that we must reject the historicity of the "decree" and deny that Paul could ever have accepted it?

There are real problems here. I do not claim to be able to solve them all. Any position which I or any other student may state is open to serious objections. In what I am about to say I do not claim that I have found a solution that will quiet all these objections. I may be adding one more weak theory to an already over-crowded line of attempted explanations. But I wish to argue that the situation has been misunderstood because the background has not been accurately discerned. The idea that Paul was forced into a tragic compromise which made impossible the maintaining of his free gospel of grace rests upon an assumption which we have no right to make.

Let me get at the issue in the following way: What happened when the first Gentiles believed in Jesus Christ? When their first church supper was planned—and remember that it was the Lord's Supper and that the Lord's Supper was a hunger-satisfying meal—did these first Gentile Christians go right out and buy a pork roast or a ham for the meat? This is what many who speak about the agreement at the Jerusalem conference seem to assume. They take it for granted that the Gentile churches from the start paid no regard to what we call "kosher food rules." The Gentile converts are supposed to have eaten whatever their previous pagan customs suggested to them. Then when Paul and the other leaders discussed at Jerusalem what should be expected or required of Gentile Christians, it would have seemed to these Gentiles an unwarranted and troublesome restriction to have to begin to respect what Jews in the church might prefer. They could have said, "We have always eaten just what we wanted to eat; no one has ever told us to do otherwise; Paul never suggested any other menu for our church suppers; why all this sudden concern for kosher rules and Jewish feelings? Are we not free in Christ? This is making slaves of us."

I have never heard this dilemma stated in this way. But I think a great many New Testament scholars have unconsciously assumed that the earliest Gentile converts, down to the time of the so-called "decree" of Acts 15:29, observed no customs intended to show deference to the feelings of Jewish believers. The validity of such an unconscious assumption must be challenged. When that is done, the whole problem takes on a different appearance.

What *did* the first Gentile Christians do about their menu at church suppers? At least a large part of them had had some contact with the synagogue. They were accustomed to the Jewish view that Gentiles who wanted to have social relations with the Jews were to abstain from practices and foods most offensive to Jews.[1] These Gentiles now came into churches where Jews were included in the number of believers. The Jews with whom they worshiped and enjoyed Christian fellowship were accustomed to follow the ceremonial laws of the Mosaic Law. Even if they

1. The rabbis said that seven commandments, "precepts of Noah," were to be kept by Gentiles. Resident aliens in Jewish territory were supposed to keep them. The seven commands prohibited: (1) worship of other gods; (2) blaspheming the name of God; (3) cursing judges; (4) murder; (5) incest and adultery; (6) robbery; (7) eating flesh with the blood of life in it; see George Foot Moore, *Judaism in the First Centuries of the Christian Era,* Vol. I (Cambridge: Harvard University Press, 1932), pp. 274-275, 339. Commands 1, 5, and 7 are paralleled in Acts 15:29.

did not expect to be saved by keeping those rules, they were used to such regulations; it was the pattern of life and worship which they continued to follow; even Paul the Apostle lived in that pattern part of the time and did so with a clear conscience (1 Cor. 9:20).

Gentile Christians who came from a previous period of association with synagogue Jews would naturally continue to think of the sensitivities of their Jewish fellow Christians. They would not follow the Mosaic Law in all respects—not by any means—but they would keep some regulations which would show respect and friendship for their Jewish fellow Christians.

When Gentiles who had never had any real tie with the synagogue came into the church, they found there both Jews who were accustomed to observe Jewish food laws and other Gentiles who were following some practices and avoiding others in order not to offend their Jewish fellow Christians. It seems to me a safe assumption that prior to the Jerusalem conference there was no church which did not include Jewish believers. The deference to Jewish feelings, I would assume, was therefore practiced throughout the church.

When Paul founded a church in which Gentiles were included, I would take it for granted that the menu at the common meals showed some concern for the Jewish believers in the group. I would assume that Paul approved and encouraged such deference. He did not think, nor did his comrades at the common table need to think, that this deference was a legal requirement which must be fulfilled as a condition of salvation.

When the Jerusalem conference was held, things were getting increasingly difficult for the Jewish Christians. They were under fire from other Jews for being traitors to their Jewish heritage. Stephen had been stoned and his Hellenistic group had been driven from the city; James the son of Zebedee had been martyred; Peter could no longer stay in Jerusalem and preach. James the brother of Jesus was generally acceptable, but he also was too liberal for almost all Jews and even for some Jewish Christians.

It was to the credit of the conference that all of the leaders nevertheless agreed that the Gentiles did not need to be circumcised to be full members of the church. It was to their credit that they did not ask for a general keeping of the ceremonial Law. The Gentile mission was approved, and the freedom of Gentile Christians from the Jewish ceremonial Law was recognized. The Gentiles, coming into the church "in the last days" (Acts 2:17), did not need to keep that Law.

If, then, in this situation Jewish Christian leaders asked and Paul agreed that Gentile Christians should be formally told that they should show some consideration for their Jewish Christian brothers, we can understand the diplomatic desirability of this in view of heavy Jewish pressure on Jewish Christian members of the church. And if Paul, as I have suggested, had been in the practice of guiding his Gentile Christians to respect the feelings of Jewish Christians and avoid glaring disregard of such feelings, there would have been nothing essentially new in what was stated as the proper practice of Gentile churches. When Paul insisted in Galatians 2:6 that the Jerusalem leaders of repute (James, Cephas, and John) "added nothing to me," he would have been stating a fact.

The problem has always been how to reconcile Paul's statement that the Jerusalem leaders "added nothing to me" with the new terms of the "decree" or decision at the conference. I suggest that this misstates the problem, since the common practice in churches containing both Jewish and Gentile believers had always been to use a menu which would give a minimum of offense to Jewish believers in the group. Food sacrificed to idols would be revolting to a Jew; meat killed in a way that left blood in it would be equally revolting; meat of fowls or animals killed by strangling likewise violated Jewish laws and feelings; and unchastity, while it may in this situation refer to marriage within forbidden degrees of relationship or to general sexual immorality, may very well refer, at least in part, to the sexual orgies at feasts in honor of pagan gods and goddesses. For Gentiles to keep away from idolatrous and immoral feasts and to avoid the eating of blood would facilitate Jewish-Gentile fellowship in the church and also promote the moral integrity which true faith in the Christian God involves.

Let me repeat that in proposing this simple—perhaps too simple—explanation of the relation between Acts 15:1-29 and Galatians 2:1-10 I do not claim to have removed all difficulties. It is quite possible, to say the least, that Luke, and perhaps other Christians, viewed the decision given in Acts 15:29 in too legalistic a way. That could help to explain why Paul later dropped it from his teaching and pastoral counsel. I have wanted to make the point that Paul won the great victory at the conference, that James the brother of Jesus, as well as Peter and John and the other Jerusalem leaders, agreed with him, and that the reasonably conjectured previous practice by which Paul and the Gentile churches accommodated their church supper menus to Jewish feelings means that the agreement reached at the Jerusalem conference did not introduce anything radically new.

VI

Conclusion

Without attempting to summarize in detail the preceding discussion, it may be helpful to list some noteworthy conclusions which have emerged:

Though Luke was limited in knowledge and himself composed the "sermons" of Acts on the basis of such information as was available to him, his history of the early church, when examined in the light of his purpose, proves essentially consistent and reliable.

Luke did not attempt to write a complete history of the Apostolic Age; in particular, he tells little of the life and growth of the individual churches; but he gives a good sketch of the rise and expansion of the church, which is the new Israel, the true Israel, entitled to official protection and popular respect.

The author of the book of Acts intended to write history in the light of God's action and purpose; he also intended to defend the church and its key leaders, especially Paul, against unjustified attacks and slanders.

The book of Acts was the key book in the formation of the New Testament canon. With the Gospel of Luke, by the same author, it linked together the Gospels and the Letters and, in particular, gave the background for the inclusion of the Letters of Paul.

The gospel for Luke was not merely a life of Jesus of Nazareth; it was the story of God's saving action for the benefit of sinful men, a story which had its background and preparatory stage in God's dealings with Israel, its center in Jesus' life, death, Resurrection, exaltation, and Lordship, and its authoritative witness in the message of the Apostles.

The preaching and the teaching of the Apostles were not mutually exclusive activities but were interrelated aspects of the basic Christian witness.

The book of Acts, and especially its sermons, do not mean to belittle the significance of Jesus' earthly ministry and the tradition about him; in the book of Acts Luke assumes the material he has given in the Gospel; the gospel of Jesus Christ the risen Lord includes and interprets the story of the ministry of Jesus.

The earliest disciples had no clear idea of the way in which the gospel was to be carried to the world, but they thought of their task not as a merely national witness to Jews but as the preaching of a gospel which had world scope.

All of the outstanding leaders of the early church, including Peter and even James the brother of Jesus, approved the Gentile mission, and Peter was active at one key stage in moving toward it. The leaders were not explicit about this mission from the first day of the church; not all of them actively took part in preaching to Gentiles; but within a generation all agreed that such preaching was to be done without requiring Gentiles to observe the Mosaic Law.

The eschatological expectation that at the end of the age the Gentiles would find a place in God's Kingdom helps to explain this world outlook of the early church.

During the Apostolic Age Jerusalem was the geographical center of the church and served to give the church a sense of unity, but the role of the Jerusalem church diminished in importance as the range of the Gentile mission widened and the stubborn hostility of the Jews to that mission increased.

The Twelve, and especially Peter, had the crucial human role in the foundation and first witness of the church; their testimony to the life, the teaching, the death, and the Resurrection of Jesus was indispensable and permanently basic.

This founding role of Peter and the Twelve was exercised mainly in the early years of the church at Jerusalem and in Palestine. As the church expanded, others took the initiative in the Gentile mission. The Twelve played a decreasing role, and they appointed no successors. Peter's later work was mainly as a missionary to the Jews.

In the Jewish Christian church at Jerusalem, James the brother of Jesus emerged as the strongest leader during the latter half of Acts. That wing of the church, by faithful respect for the Mosaic Law, won many Jews, but when it lost its center in Jerusalem it lost contact with the Gentile church, and while it continued its ministry among Jews for several centuries, it met with diminishing success.

The development of the church from a group composed entirely of Jews to a world church containing both Jews and Gentiles was spearheaded by the Hellenists, who spoke Greek, had some knowledge of the Gentile world, and were able best to bridge the gap between Jewish Christians and the Gentile world. These Hellenists were in the church at Jerusalem in its earliest days.

While Stephen did not himself break out of the traditional forms of Judaism, his free spirit, championing insights received from Jesus, prepared the way for the Gentile mission.

Philip was perhaps less vigorous and creative than Stephen, but his preaching of the gospel in Samaria was an important step in the movement toward a full mission to Gentiles.

In the early stages of the preaching of the gospel to the Gentiles, Barnabas had a key role. Trusted by the Jerusalem church, able to win the confidence of the integrated church at Antioch, and quick to discern the genuine conversion and potential gifts of Paul, he was highly influential in the emergence of the Gentile mission.

For Luke, Paul was the outstanding figure of the story of Acts. He is on stage more than twice as much as Peter; in fact, he appears as much as all the other church leaders put together, and in the latter half of the book he dominates the story in a remarkable way.

The general movement of the expansion of the church is toward Rome; the church's presence there is a symbol of its world mission; Peter has no place in the bringing of the gospel to Rome or in the leadership of the Roman church in the period covered by Acts; it is Paul who gives that church apostolic standing by coming to Rome and preaching there.

The book of Acts prescribes no rigid doctrinal statement or form of church organization. Its view is that all of the apostolic leaders preached one gospel, and that the Holy Spirit guided the church to find the patterns of organization and life suited to express the Christian faith and further the Christian witness.

This freedom was disciplined by brotherly concern for fellow Christians. The Jewish Christians conceded that Gentile Christians need not keep the Mosaic Law, and the Gentile Christians were willing to observe conciliating practices which demonstrated their break with paganism and their respect for Jewish Christians who felt bound to observe the Mosaic Law.